The Great American Documents

VOLUME I: 1620–1830

UNCLE SAM

PRESENTS

The Great American Documents

VOLUME I: 1620–1830

Ruth Ashby

ILLUSTRATED BY

Ernie Colón

EDITORIAL CONSULTANT

Russell Motter

A NOVEL GRAPHIC from HILL AND WANG
A DIVISION OF FARRAR, STRAUS AND GIROUX
NEW YORK

To Calder and Lachlan

Hill and Wang
A division of Farrar, Straus and Giroux
18 West 18th Street, New York 10011

This is a Z File, Inc. Book
Text copyright © 2014 by Ruth Ashby
Artwork copyright © 2014 by Ernie Colón
All rights reserved
Printed in the United States of America
Published simultaneously in hardcover and paperback
First edition, 2014

Library of Congress Control Number: 2013956401
Hardcover ISBN: 978-0-8090-9460-8
Paperback ISBN: 978-0-374-53453-0

Hill and Wang books may be purchased for educational, business, or
promotional use. For information on bulk purchases, please contact the
Macmillan Corporate and Premium Sales Department at 1-800-221-7945,
extension 5442, or write to specialmarkets@macmillan.com.

Editor: Howard Zimmerman
Editorial Consultant: Russell Motter
Designer: Richard Amari

www.fsgbooks.com
www.twitter.com/fsgbooks • www.facebook.com/fsgbooks

1 3 5 7 9 10 8 6 4 2

INTRODUCTION

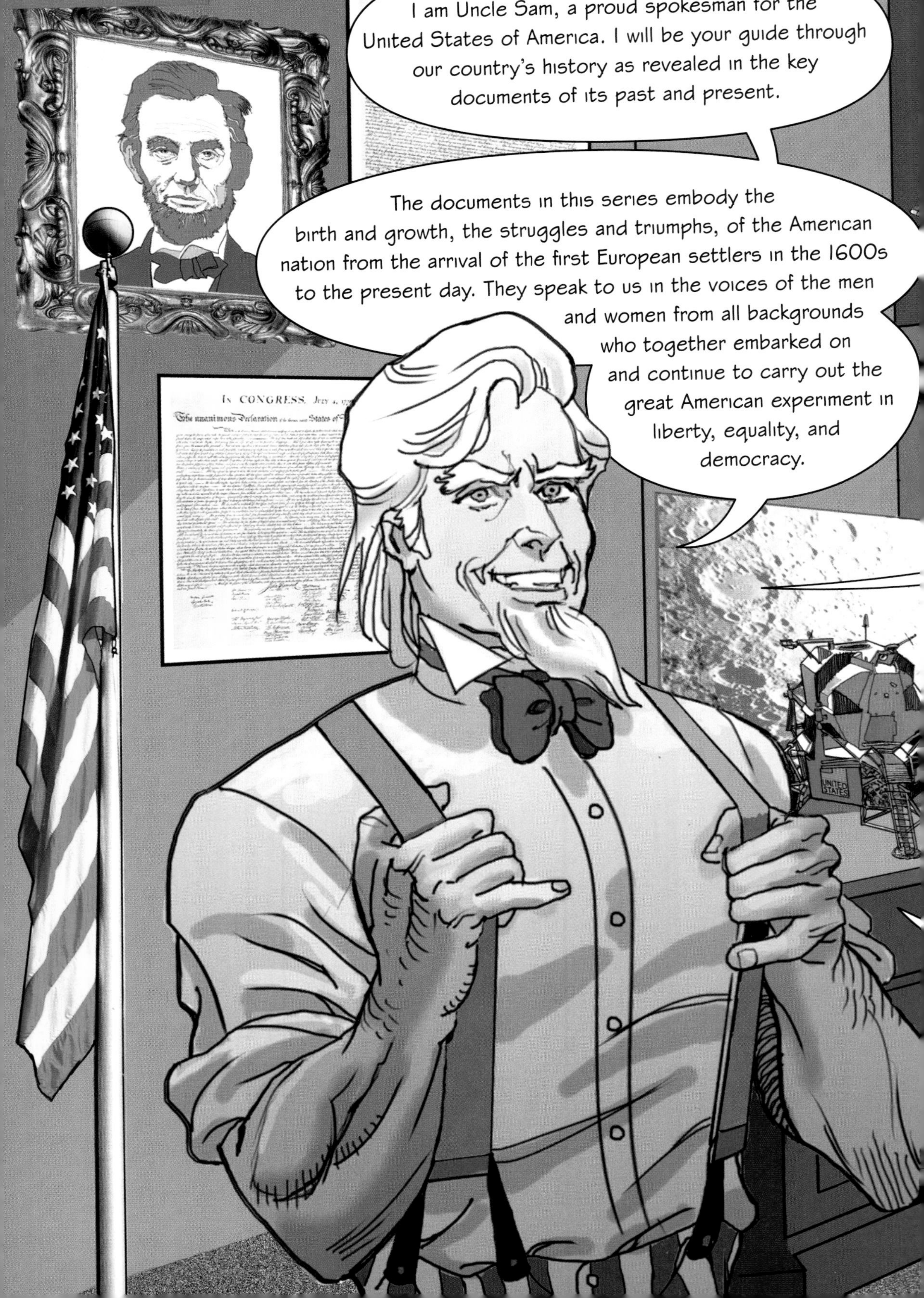
I am Uncle Sam, a proud spokesman for the United States of America. I will be your guide through our country's history as revealed in the key documents of its past and present.
The documents in this series embody the birth and growth, the struggles and triumphs, of the American nation from the arrival of the first European settlers in the 1600s to the present day. They speak to us in the voices of the men and women from all backgrounds who together embarked on and continue to carry out the great American experiment in liberty, equality, and democracy.

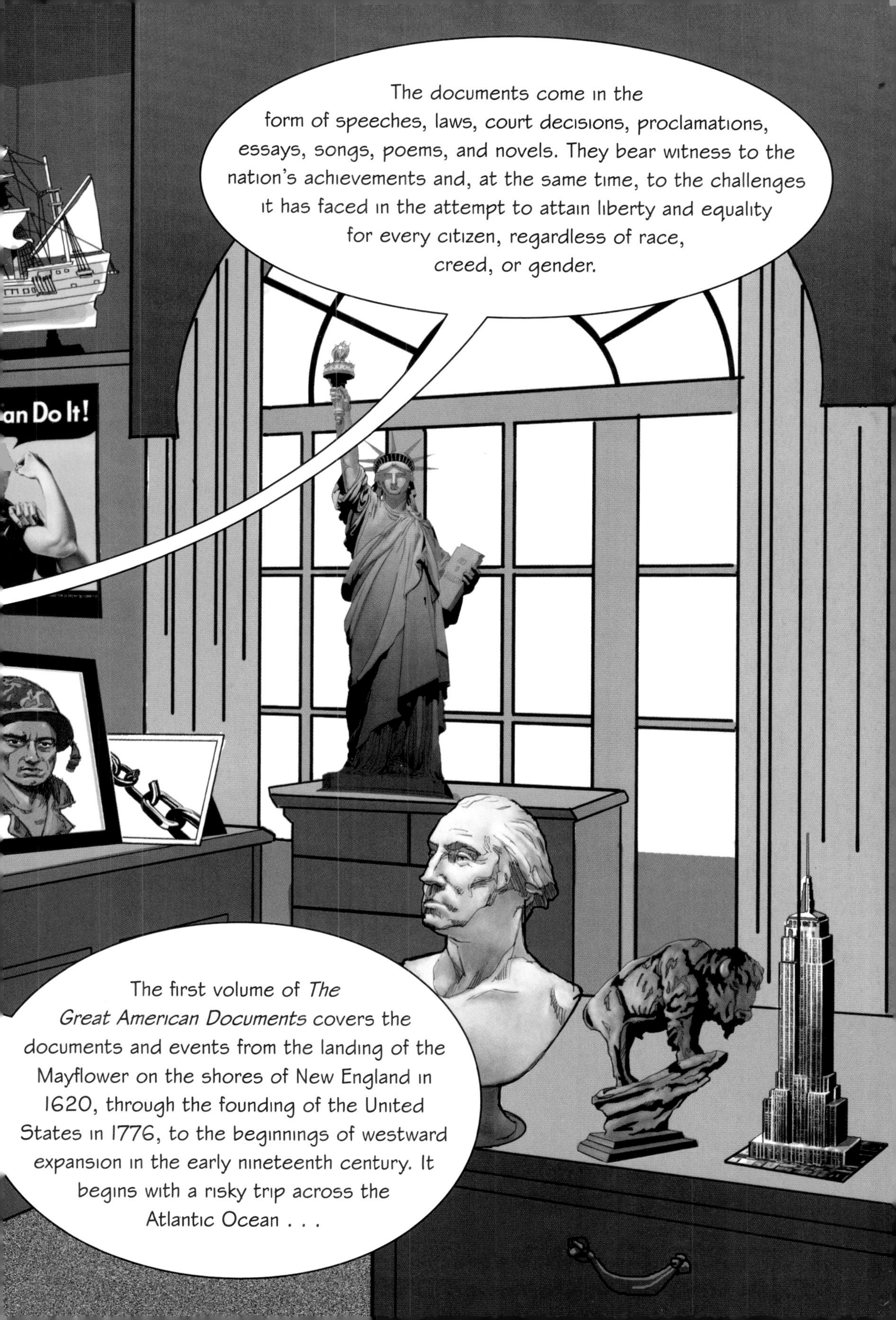
The documents come in the form of speeches, laws, court decisions, proclamations, essays, songs, poems, and novels. They bear witness to the nation's achievements and, at the same time, to the challenges it has faced in the attempt to attain liberty and equality for every citizen, regardless of race, creed, or gender.
an Do It!
The first volume of *The Great American Documents* covers the documents and events from the landing of the Mayflower on the shores of New England in 1620, through the founding of the United States in 1776, to the beginnings of westward expansion in the early nineteenth century. It begins with a risky trip across the Atlantic Ocean . . .

The Mayflower Compact

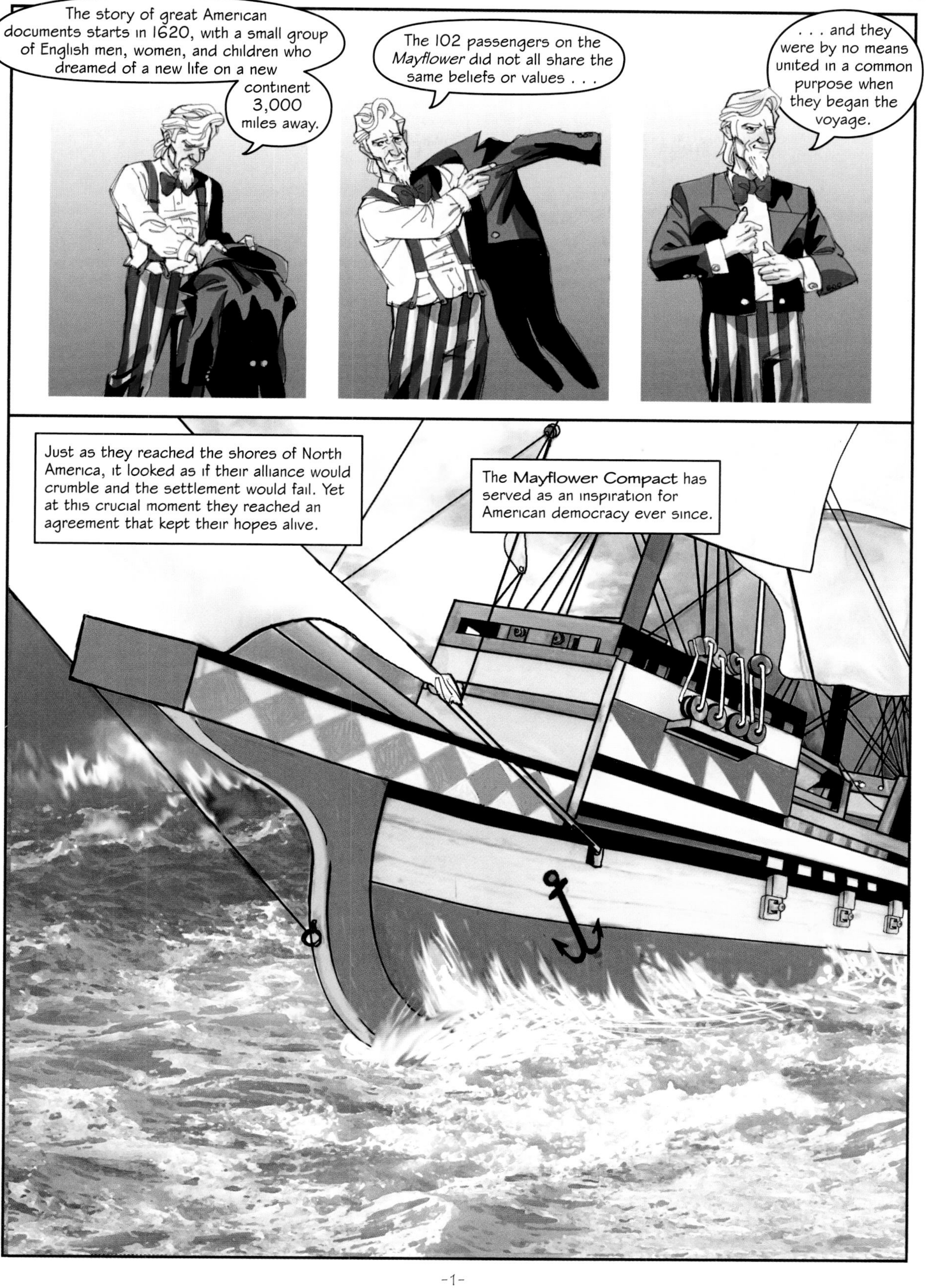

The story of great American documents starts in 1620, with a small group of English men, women, and children who dreamed of a new life on a new continent 3,000 miles away.
The 102 passengers on the *Mayflower* did not all share the same beliefs or values . . .
. . . and they were by no means united in a common purpose when they began the voyage.
Just as they reached the shores of North America, it looked as if their alliance would crumble and the settlement would fail. Yet at this crucial moment they reached an agreement that kept their hopes alive.
The Mayflower Compact has served as an inspiration for American democracy ever since.

The court of King James I, 1604.

It was a time of religious turmoil throughout Europe. The English king, James I, was also head of his state's religion, Anglicanism, and he insisted that all English men and women join it.

But while some wanted to work to make the Anglican Church better, many others wanted nothing to do with it. The king was not pleased.

THESE SEPARATISTS HOLD SECRET MEETINGS AND DEFY YOUR LAWS, SIRE.

I WILL HAVE ONE RELIGION IN THIS COUNTRY. I SHALL MAKE THEM CONFORM THEMSELVES OR I SHALL HOUND THEM FROM THE LAND!

The village of Scrooby, England, 1606.

William Brewster and others established a secret congregation of Separatists. They wished to practice their own form of Christianity rather than that dictated by the king.

OUR COVENANT IS WITH GOD.

AND WITH THIS COMMUNITY OF BELIEVERS!

BANG! BANG! BANG!

But the king's agents kept track of those who would defy his orders.

WILLIAM BREWSTER, I ARREST YOU IN THE NAME OF THE KING!

WE PUT OUR FAITH IN THE LORD.

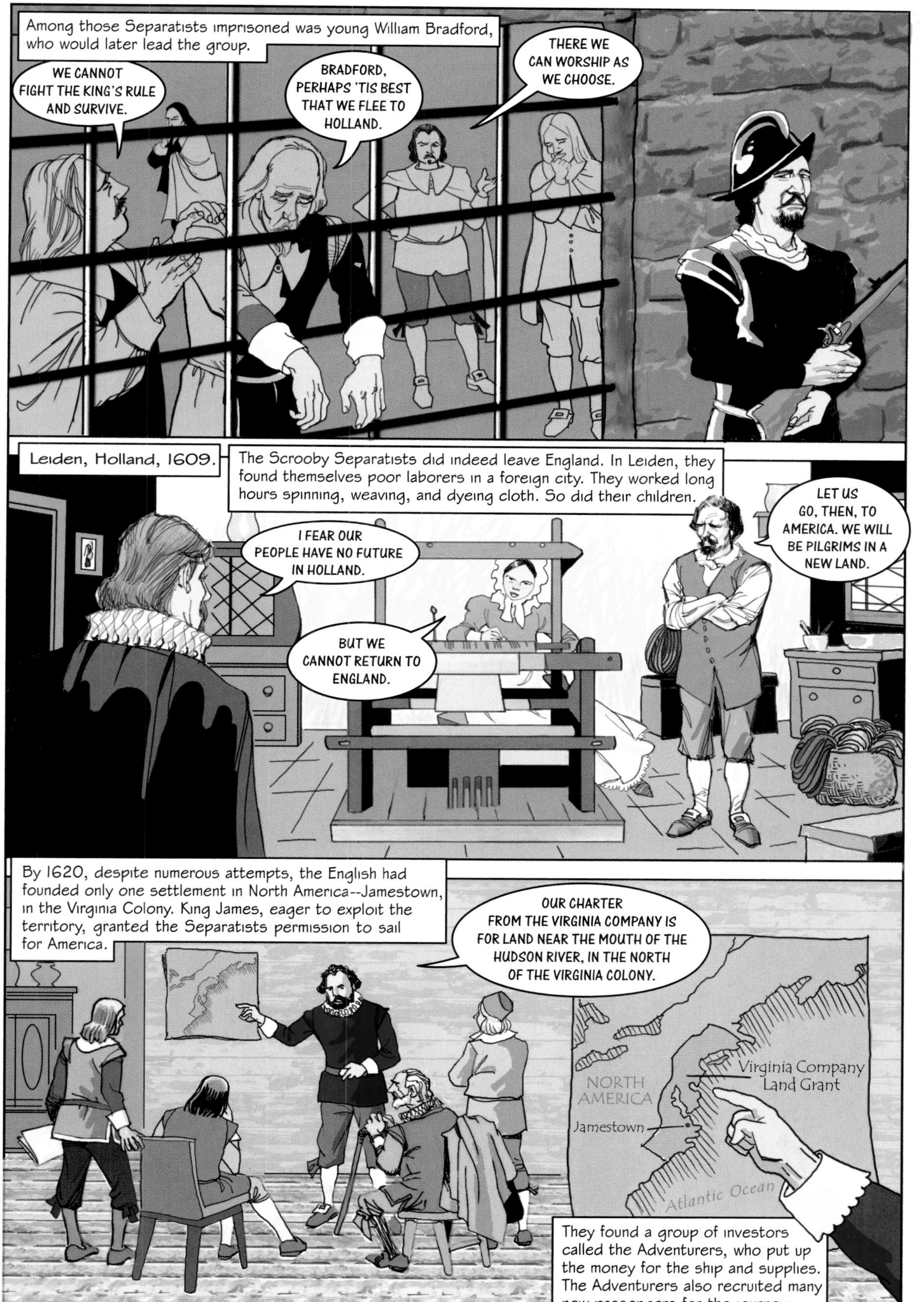
Among those Separatists imprisoned was young William Bradford, who would later lead the group.
WE CANNOT FIGHT THE KING'S RULE AND SURVIVE.
BRADFORD, PERHAPS 'TIS BEST THAT WE FLEE TO HOLLAND.
THERE WE CAN WORSHIP AS WE CHOOSE.
Leiden, Holland, 1609.
The Scrooby Separatists did indeed leave England. In Leiden, they found themselves poor laborers in a foreign city. They worked long hours spinning, weaving, and dyeing cloth. So did their children.
I FEAR OUR PEOPLE HAVE NO FUTURE IN HOLLAND.
BUT WE CANNOT RETURN TO ENGLAND.
LET US GO, THEN, TO AMERICA. WE WILL BE PILGRIMS IN A NEW LAND.
By 1620, despite numerous attempts, the English had founded only one settlement in North America--Jamestown, in the Virginia Colony. King James, eager to exploit the territory, granted the Separatists permission to sail for America.
OUR CHARTER FROM THE VIRGINIA COMPANY IS FOR LAND NEAR THE MOUTH OF THE HUDSON RIVER, IN THE NORTH OF THE VIRGINIA COLONY.
NORTH AMERICA
Virginia Company Land Grant
Jamestown
Atlantic Ocean
They found a group of investors called the Adventurers, who put up the money for the ship and supplies. The Adventurers also recruited many new passengers for the journey.

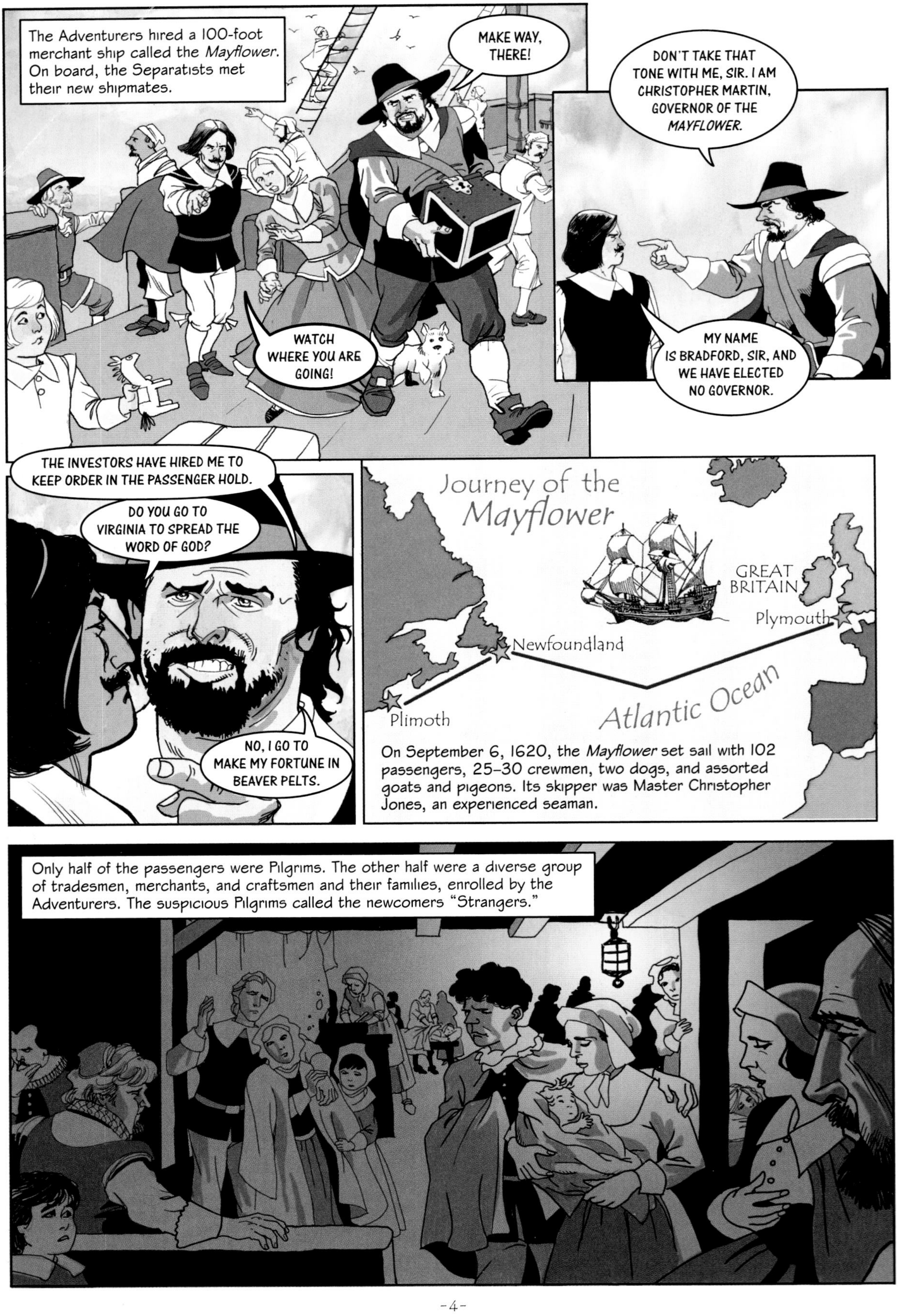
The Adventurers hired a 100-foot merchant ship called the *Mayflower*. On board, the Separatists met their new shipmates.
MAKE WAY, THERE!
WATCH WHERE YOU ARE GOING!
DON'T TAKE THAT TONE WITH ME, SIR. I AM CHRISTOPHER MARTIN, GOVERNOR OF THE *MAYFLOWER*.
MY NAME IS BRADFORD, SIR, AND WE HAVE ELECTED NO GOVERNOR.
THE INVESTORS HAVE HIRED ME TO KEEP ORDER IN THE PASSENGER HOLD.
DO YOU GO TO VIRGINIA TO SPREAD THE WORD OF GOD?
NO, I GO TO MAKE MY FORTUNE IN BEAVER PELTS.
Journey of the *Mayflower*
GREAT BRITAIN
Plymouth
Newfoundland
Atlantic Ocean
Plimoth
On September 6, 1620, the *Mayflower* set sail with 102 passengers, 25–30 crewmen, two dogs, and assorted goats and pigeons. Its skipper was Master Christopher Jones, an experienced seaman.
Only half of the passengers were Pilgrims. The other half were a diverse group of tradesmen, merchants, and craftsmen and their families, enrolled by the Adventurers. The suspicious Pilgrims called the newcomers "Strangers."

As autumn storms battered the ship, passengers huddled belowdecks, seasick and terrified.

The storms swept the *Mayflower* far north of the Hudson River, toward the shores of New England.

On November 9, 1620, off the banks of Cape Cod . . .

LAND HO!

BEAR SOUTH ALONG THE COAST, TOWARD THE HUDSON RIVER.

Yet shoals and sandbars lurking beneath the surface of the water threatened to run the *Mayflower* aground and break her up.

WE SHALL ALL PERISH!

ARE NOT WE CLOSE TO LAND?

THESE ARE RISKY WATERS, INDEED.

TURN BACK! WE CANNOT RISK A SHIPWRECK. WE WILL RETURN NORTH TO *CAPE COD*.

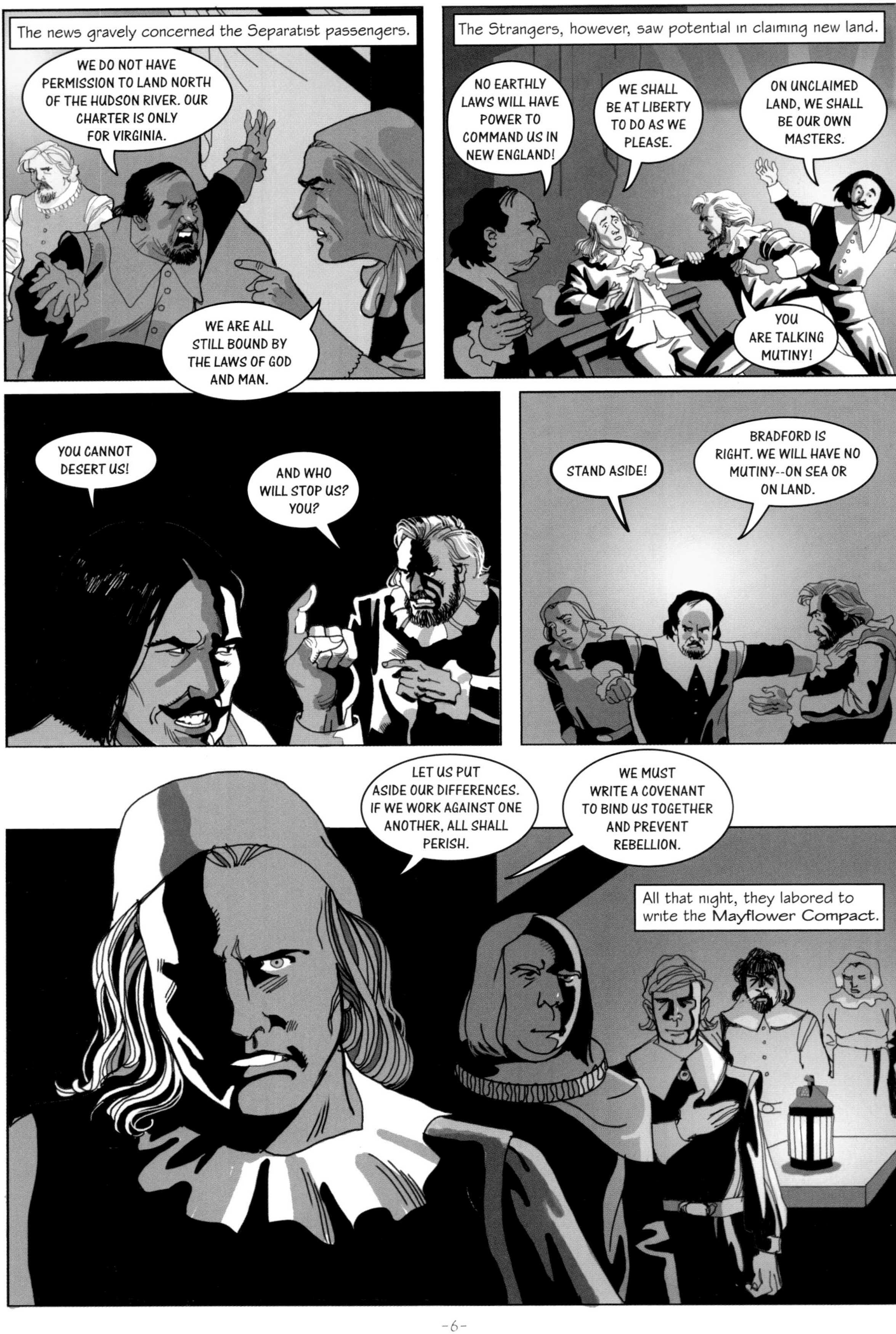
The news gravely concerned the Separatist passengers.
WE DO NOT HAVE PERMISSION TO LAND NORTH OF THE HUDSON RIVER. OUR CHARTER IS ONLY FOR VIRGINIA.
WE ARE ALL STILL BOUND BY THE LAWS OF GOD AND MAN.
The Strangers, however, saw potential in claiming new land.
NO EARTHLY LAWS WILL HAVE POWER TO COMMAND US IN NEW ENGLAND!
WE SHALL BE AT LIBERTY TO DO AS WE PLEASE.
ON UNCLAIMED LAND, WE SHALL BE OUR OWN MASTERS.
YOU ARE TALKING MUTINY!
YOU CANNOT DESERT US!
AND WHO WILL STOP US? YOU?
STAND ASIDE!
BRADFORD IS RIGHT. WE WILL HAVE NO MUTINY--ON SEA OR ON LAND.
LET US PUT ASIDE OUR DIFFERENCES. IF WE WORK AGAINST ONE ANOTHER, ALL SHALL PERISH.
WE MUST WRITE A COVENANT TO BIND US TOGETHER AND PREVENT REBELLION.
All that night, they labored to write the Mayflower Compact.

Mayflower Common Room, November 11, 1620.

The next morning, passengers gathered for the signing ceremony.

"...These present do covenant and combine ourselves together into a civil body politic..."

One by one, 41 men signed their names.

HUZZAH!

Later that day, the first group ventured ashore.

PRAISE GOD, WHO HAS DELIVERED US FROM THE VAST AND FURIOUS OCEAN.

A month later, the *Mayflower*'s voyagers founded their colony at Plymouth Harbor. During the winter of 1620–21, more than half of the original settlers would die from hardship, starvation, and disease.

The local Indians taught the survivors what to eat and how to farm this new land. In autumn of 1621, Pilgrims and Indians came together for a harvest feast.

William Bradford served as governor of Plymouth Colony for 31 years. The colony also had a general court with representatives from various communities. Town meetings of male citizens would debate issues and try to resolve problems.

The model developed at Plymouth and other New England colonies would influence the formation of the United States government 150 years later.

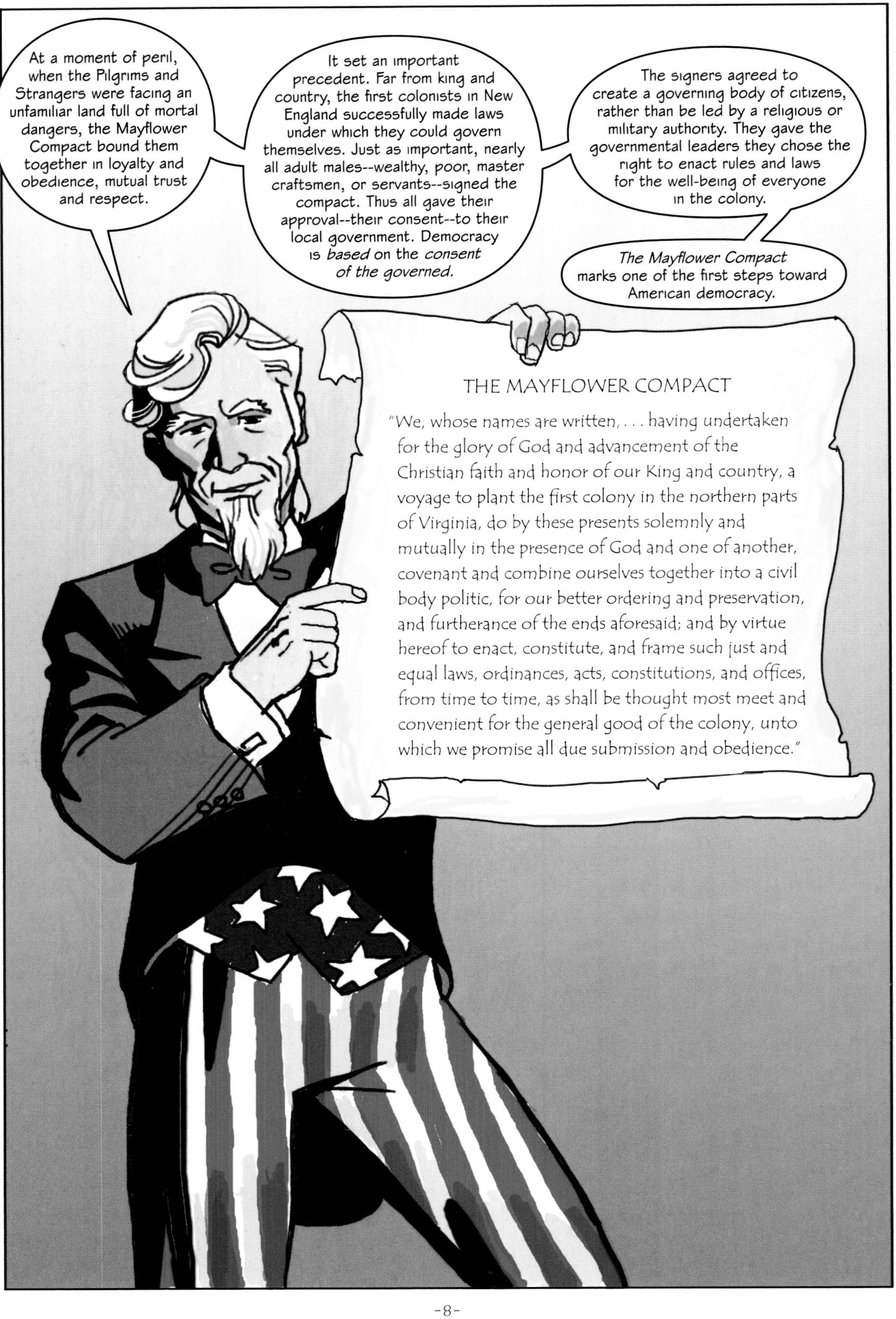

At a moment of peril, when the Pilgrims and Strangers were facing an unfamiliar land full of mortal dangers, the Mayflower Compact bound them together in loyalty and obedience, mutual trust and respect.
It set an important precedent. Far from king and country, the first colonists in New England successfully made laws under which they could govern themselves. Just as important, nearly all adult males--wealthy, poor, master craftsmen, or servants--signed the compact. Thus all gave their approval--their consent--to their local government. Democracy is *based* on the *consent of the governed.*
The signers agreed to create a governing body of citizens, rather than be led by a religious or military authority. They gave the governmental leaders they chose the right to enact rules and laws for the well-being of everyone in the colony.
The Mayflower Compact marks one of the first steps toward American democracy.
THE MAYFLOWER COMPACT
"We, whose names are written, . . . having undertaken for the glory of God and advancement of the Christian faith and honor of our King and country, a voyage to plant the first colony in the northern parts of Virginia, do by these presents solemnly and mutually in the presence of God and one of another, covenant and combine ourselves together into a civil body politic, for our better ordering and preservation, and furtherance of the ends aforesaid; and by virtue hereof to enact, constitute, and frame such just and equal laws, ordinances, acts, constitutions, and offices, from time to time, as shall be thought most meet and convenient for the general good of the colony, unto which we promise all due submission and obedience."

Ten years after the English Separatists landed in America, they were followed by waves of immigrants who founded villages up and down the New England coast.

Driven by a combination of idealism and single-minded faith, these new arrivals risked everything to make their dream of a perfect community come true. They believed they had a holy mission to create a model Christian society based on the Bible.

In 1629, a group of wealthy Puritan merchants--led by John Winthrop--obtained a charter from the new king of England, Charles I, to colonize what is now New Hampshire, southern Maine, and most of Massachusetts.

WE SHALL CARRY THE WORD OF GOD TO AMERICA! FOR WE ARE HIS CHOSEN PEOPLE.

Southampton, England, March 1630.

Winthrop, the newly elected governor of the Massachusetts Bay Colony, delivered a statement of principles called A Model of Christian Charity to those sailing with him to New England.

He said their colony would be as "a city upon a hill," a phrase used by Jesus in his Sermon on the Mount. Winthrop meant that the whole world would see if they failed or prospered and how they conducted themselves.

MASSACHUSETTS BAY COLONY

BOSTON

PLYMOUTH

GREAT BRITAIN

The news of a *great migration* swept across England. People sold homes and belongings and bade farewell. Between 1629 and 1640, about 20,000 people joined Winthrop in creating his City upon a Hill.

Massachusetts Bay, 1634.

Among the most enthusiastic were the smart and tough 43-year-old Anne Hutchinson, her husband, Will, and ten of their children.

They joined a tightly knit community in which all members were required to work together for the common good.

They were all expected to attend the same church services . . .

. . . obey the same strict rules of behavior and dress or face the penalty of public punishment . . .

SHE WAS GOSSIPING ABOUT HER NEIGHBORS!

AND IN THE CHURCH!

. . . and submit to the authority of ministers and government officials.

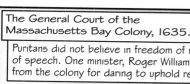

The General Court of the Massachusetts Bay Colony, 1635.

Puritans did not believe in freedom of religion or freedom of speech. One minister, Roger Williams, was banished from the colony for daring to uphold religious *tolerance*.

Williams trekked to Narragansett Bay and founded Providence, where he and his followers welcomed people of diverse faiths.

November 1637. Anne Hutchinson was also summoned before the General Court and charged with holding Bible classes in her home.

YOU HAVE TROUBLED THE PEACE OF THE COMMONWEALTH. YOU HAVE SPOKEN AGAINST THE HONOR OF THE CHURCHES AND MINISTERS.

AND YOU HAVE MAINTAINED A MEETING IN YOUR HOUSE THAT IS NOT TOLERABLE IN THE SIGHT OF GOD NOR FITTING FOR YOUR SEX.

I DO *NOT* BELIEVE THIS TO BE SO.

WE ARE YOUR JUDGES--YOU ARE NOT OURS.

HOW DO YOU KNOW THAT IT WAS *GOD* THAT DID REVEAL YOUR IDEAS TO YOU?

BY THE VOICE OF HIS OWN SPIRIT TO MY SOUL.

Hutchinson's claim that God spoke *directly to her* sealed her fate. How dare anyone other than a minister--let alone a woman--interpret the word of God?

The General Court--all men--were outraged.

YOU ARE A WOMAN NOT FIT FOR OUR SOCIETY. WE *BANISH* YOU FROM OUR LAND.

Hutchinson escaped with her family, first to Williams's Providence, then to the Dutch colony of New Netherland. There, she and all but one of her seven youngest children were massacred during a war between the Dutch and the local Indians.

Puritans successfully suppressed dissent in their community, though innocent people paid the price with their freedom, and sometimes with their lives.

The Massachusetts Bay Colony flourished. Settlers founded Harvard College and the first public schools in America. Together, farmers, merchants, and fishermen turned Winthrop's "City upon a Hill" into a model of industry, trade, and prosperity.

Winthrop envisioned a community so closely knit that it would be "as one man." Citizens would be totally supportive of one another. They would also *all* hold the same religious and moral beliefs.

Although Winthrop and other officials were not clergymen, the *government* and the Puritan *ministers* cooperated fully. The relationship between church and state was so close that the Massachusetts Bay Colony is often called a theocracy.

The idea that the United States has a special mission is known as American exceptionalism. President Ronald Reagan often used the image of the city upon a hill to illustrate his belief that the nation should shine like a beacon to freedom-seeking people everywhere.

EXCERPT FROM
A MODEL OF CHRISTIAN CHARITY

"We must be knit together in this work as one man . . . We shall find that the God of Israel is among us, when ten of us shall be able to resist a thousand of our enemies, when He shall make of us a praise and glory so that men shall say of succeeding plantations, 'The Lord make it like that of New England,' for we must consider that we shall be as a city upon a hill, the eyes of all people are upon us. So that if we shall deal falsely with our God in this work we have undertaken, and so cause Him to withdraw His present help from us, we shall be made a story and a by-word through the world."

The Maryland Toleration Act

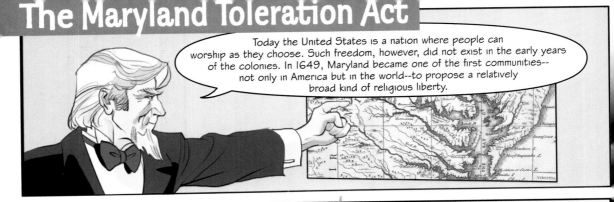

Today the United States is a nation where people can worship as they choose. Such freedom, however, did not exist in the early years of the colonies. In 1649, Maryland became one of the first communities-- not only in America but in the world--to propose a relatively broad kind of religious liberty.

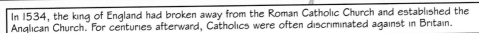

In 1534, the king of England had broken away from the Roman Catholic Church and established the Anglican Church. For centuries afterward, Catholics were often discriminated against in Britain.

KING HENRY VIII

POPE CLEMENT VII

In the 1600s, England was a battleground of opposing Christian faiths. Anglican, Roman Catholic, Puritan, Separatist, Quaker--each claimed to be the *one true religion*, and all were intolerant of the others.

I'M RIGHT, YOU'RE WRONG!

RELIGION

HATE YOUR RELIGION

Catholic families sometimes "conformed" to Anglicanism so they could keep their wealth and influence. George Calvert, Lord Baltimore, was a Catholic minister at court who only remained such because he *conformed*. But in 1625 . . .

I WOULD LIKE TO TENDER MY RESIGNATION AS SECRETARY OF STATE. FROM THIS TIME FORWARD, I WILL BE CATHOLIC AGAIN.

Eager to embark on a new venture, Lord Baltimore conceived a bold scheme. Because of his many friends at court, he convinced King Charles I to grant him a vast tract of land on the Chesapeake Bay.

I WILL FOUND A NORTH AMERICAN COLONY WHERE CATHOLICS CAN FIND A SAFE HAVEN.

1634. Two ships, the *Ark* and the *Dove*, carrying about 150 colonists, arrived in Mary's Land. Most were Protestants . . . some were Catholics. On March 25, Father Andrew White celebrated their safe arrival.

But in the 1640s, England erupted in civil war. Puritan Roundheads, who supported Parliament, fought the king's Cavaliers over power and religion . . .

. . . and in America, Puritans from Virginia invaded the colony of Mary's Land and drove Lord Baltimore's Catholics from power.

Baltimore's son Cecil sent in soldiers and regained control. He planned to make Maryland a place of peace and religious tolerance.

In England, the Puritans won the civil war and executed King Charles. In the aftermath, Maryland's Act of Toleration was repealed . . . then reinstated . . . then repealed again.

Not until the passage of the First Amendment to the Constitution in 1791 was religious freedom guaranteed for all American citizens.

1649. The Maryland Assembly debated Cecil's proposals, then it passed an act granting freedom of conscience to all Christians. We call it the Maryland Toleration Act.

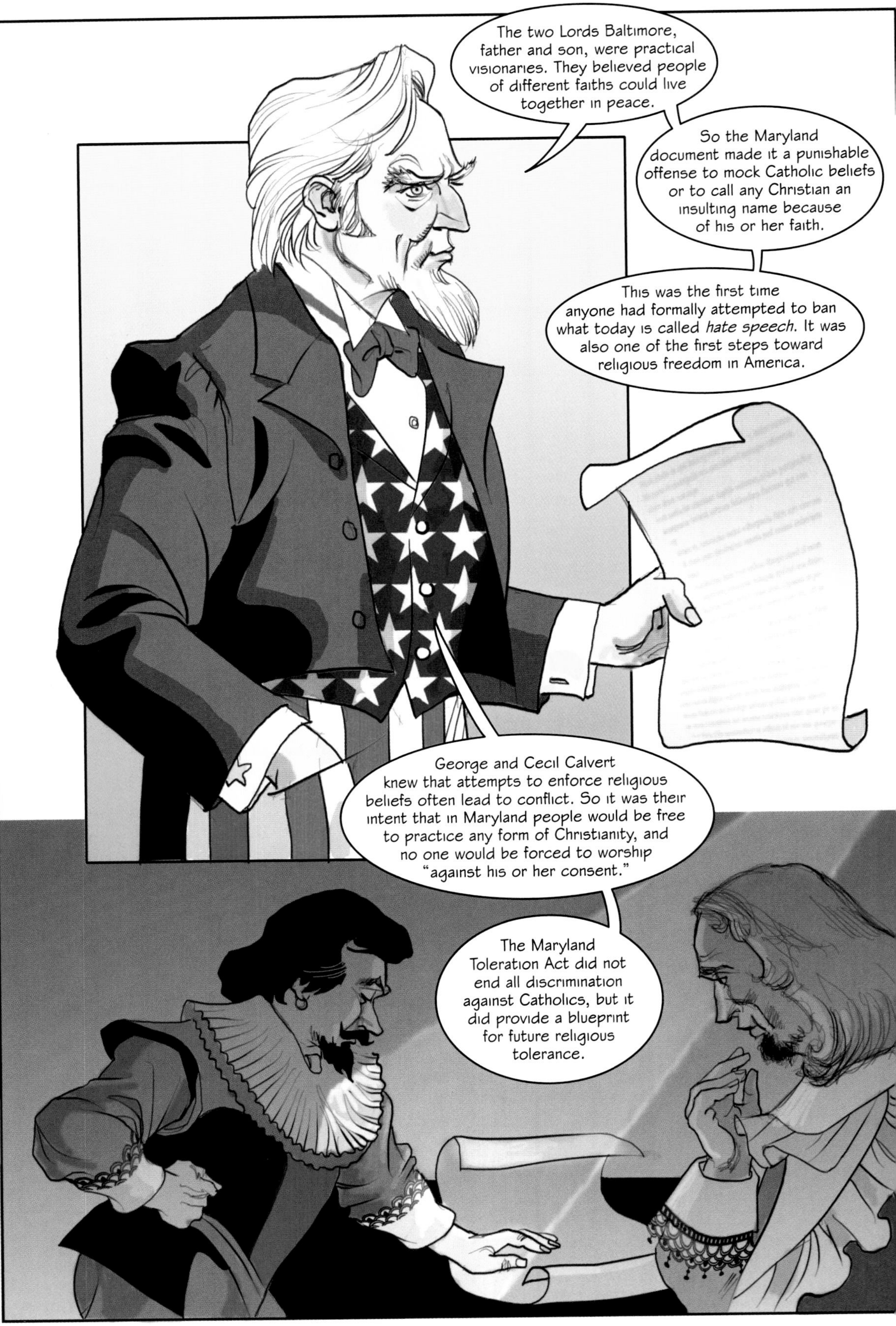
The two Lords Baltimore, father and son, were practical visionaries. They believed people of different faiths could live together in peace.
So the Maryland document made it a punishable offense to mock Catholic beliefs or to call any Christian an insulting name because of his or her faith.
This was the first time anyone had formally attempted to ban what today is called *hate speech.* It was also one of the first steps toward religious freedom in America.
George and Cecil Calvert knew that attempts to enforce religious beliefs often lead to conflict. So it was their intent that in Maryland people would be free to practice any form of Christianity, and no one would be forced to worship "against his or her consent."
The Maryland Toleration Act did not end all discrimination against Catholics, but it did provide a blueprint for future religious tolerance.

Slavery in North America began slowly in the early 1600s, with the arrival in Virginia of a few captured Africans. They joined white indentured servants and captured Indians as laborers on the farms of struggling landowners.

In the British colonies, poor people could buy passages to America by signing contracts called *indentures*. After seven years of work, they became free men and women.

Even African slaves were allowed to gain their freedom after a period of time.

But by the end of the 17th century, black servants had lost the hope of eventual freedom and were trapped in a cycle of slavery. The Virginia Slave Codes of 1705 exemplified the terrible change in their legal status.

Jamestown, Virginia, August 1619. A Dutch ship, the *White Lion*, pulled into the dock bearing 20 African slaves.

WE WILL SELL THESE MEN FOR FOOD AND SUPPLIES.

In 1621, one newly arrived prisoner was sold to the owner of a small tobacco plantation.

NAME? YOUR NAME?

ANTONIO.

ANTONIO, YOU ARE MY BOND SERVANT.

Antonio worked in the tobacco fields alongside the white indentured servants. It was backbreaking labor.

JEMMY, HOW LONG ARE YOU BOUND TO MASTER BENNETT?

SEVEN YEARS. THEN, MY FREEDOM DUES--MY OWN LAND, AND A GUN.

I WANT MY FREEDOM DUES, TOO.

In early Virginia, Antonio was called not a slave but a *servant*. Yet unlike Jemmy, he had not signed a contract that stated when he would be freed from service--if ever.

But Antonio's hard work was eventually rewarded. He became a Christian.

I BAPTIZE YOU ANTHONY JOHNSON.

He was allowed to marry the woman he loved . . .

ANTHONY AND MARY ARE NOW MAN AND WIFE.

. . . and he became a free man.

MR. BENNETT LET ME BUY MY FREEDOM!

By 1651, freeman Anthony Johnson had a 250-acre plantation of his own. Like other farmers, he had servants and slaves to help him grow and harvest tobacco.

I ORDER THE RUNAWAY SLAVE JOHN CASAR RETURNED TO THE POSSESSION OF ANTHONY JOHNSON FORTHWITH.

Anthony Johnson died in 1670. His wife, Mary, passed on ten years later. Both lived to see their grandchildren grow up free and own farms.

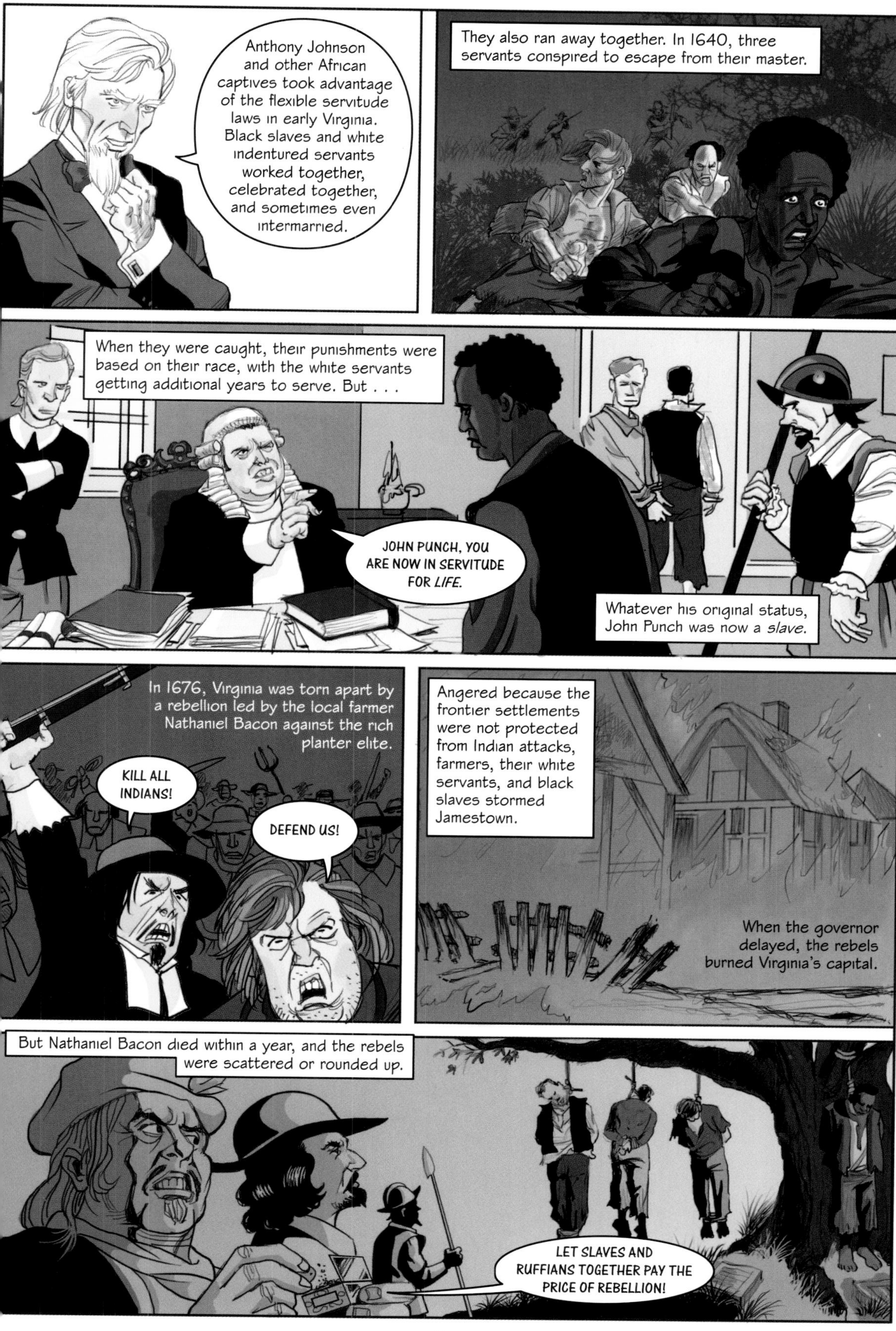

Anthony Johnson and other African captives took advantage of the flexible servitude laws in early Virginia. Black slaves and white indentured servants worked together, celebrated together, and sometimes even intermarried.
They also ran away together. In 1640, three servants conspired to escape from their master.
When they were caught, their punishments were based on their race, with the white servants getting additional years to serve. But . . .
JOHN PUNCH, YOU ARE NOW IN SERVITUDE FOR *LIFE*.
Whatever his original status, John Punch was now a *slave*.
In 1676, Virginia was torn apart by a rebellion led by the local farmer Nathaniel Bacon against the rich planter elite.
KILL ALL INDIANS!
DEFEND US!
Angered because the frontier settlements were not protected from Indian attacks, farmers, their white servants, and black slaves stormed Jamestown.
When the governor delayed, the rebels burned Virginia's capital.
But Nathaniel Bacon died within a year, and the rebels were scattered or rounded up.
LET SLAVES AND RUFFIANS TOGETHER PAY THE PRICE OF REBELLION!

Meanwhile . . .

. . . mass importation of people from Africa and Barbados to the colonies . . .

. . . transformed the fate of slaves in North America.

The Chesapeake Bay, around 1690. Robert "King" Carter, owner of 300,000 acres and 1,500 slaves, was the wealthiest of a new breed of Virginia tobacco planters.

TWENTY POUNDS FOR THIS ONE.

YOU ARE DINAH.

NKIRU!

DINAH!

Like other planters, Carter had developed an ironclad formula for success. More slave labor meant more tobacco, and more tobacco meant more money.

THIRTY LASHES WHEN YOU REFUSE TO WORK!

A decade later . . .

BUY ONLY AFRICAN SLAVES. THEY COST MORE . . . BUT YOU OWN THEM FOREVER. AND THEY FARE BETTER AGAINST THE MALARIA.

TOO MANY SLAVES MIGHT RISE UP IN REBELLION.

NO MORE INDENTURED SERVANTS FOR ME. YOU FEED THEM, CLOTHE THEM--THEN THEY'RE GONE. OR THEY CATCH MALARIA AND DIE.

NOT IF WE CONTROL THEM TOTALLY.

Carter's actions lived up to his words.

BAMBERRA HENRY AND DINAH, THIS IS YOUR THIRD ESCAPE ATTEMPT.

I KNOW HOW TO KEEP SLAVES FROM RUNNING AWAY. CUT OFF THEIR TOES!

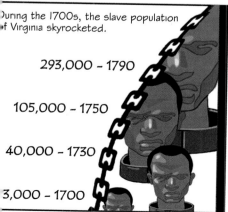

During the 1700s, the slave population of Virginia skyrocketed.

293,000 – 1790

105,000 – 1750

40,000 – 1730

3,000 – 1700

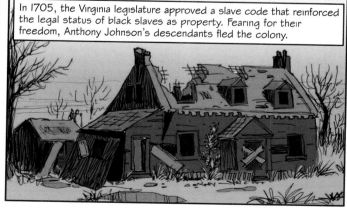

In 1705, the Virginia legislature approved a slave code that reinforced the legal status of black slaves as property. Fearing for their freedom, Anthony Johnson's descendants fled the colony.

As members of the House of Burgesses, "King" Carter and other wealthy Virginians passed laws that progressively deprived slaves of any legal rights.

Other colonies passed similar laws, especially in the South, where the economy was based on the growing of rice, tobacco, and indigo on large plantations worked by slave labor. And so the Southern slave society was born.

In Anthony Johnson's day, African servants became Christian in hopes of proving that they were part of the larger society. But under the new slave codes, conversion would no longer save them from a life of bondage.

Owners could maim or even kill their slaves without fear of punishment. And by making children's slave status dependent on the status of the mother rather than the father, the law ensured that slavery would continue from generation to generation.

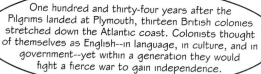

One hundred and thirty-four years after the Pilgrims landed at Plymouth, thirteen British colonies stretched down the Atlantic coast. Colonists thought of themselves as English--in language, in culture, and in government--yet within a generation they would fight a fierce war to gain independence.

What happened? To understand, we can look at another war that blazed across the continent for nine long years. Called by Americans the French and Indian War, it expanded the boundaries of British territory and, in the Albany Plan of Union, planted the seeds of eventual cooperation among the colonies.

Oh, and it also introduced a future United States president to the world stage.

THIRTEEN COLONIES

New Hampshire
MAINE (part of MA)
Massachusetts
New York
Rhode Island
Connecticut
New Jersey
Delaware
Pennsylvania
Virginia
Maryland
North Carolina
South Carolina
Georgia

Atlantic Ocean

Ohio River Valley, May 28, 1754. A group of Virginia militia, led by an inexperienced officer, stumbled across French soldiers encamped in the woods. Britain and France were not presently at war. Yet within minutes . . .

FIRE!

. . . without meaning to, young George Washington started the French and Indian War. "The volley fired by this young Virginian in the forests of America," an English writer remarked, "has set the world on fire."

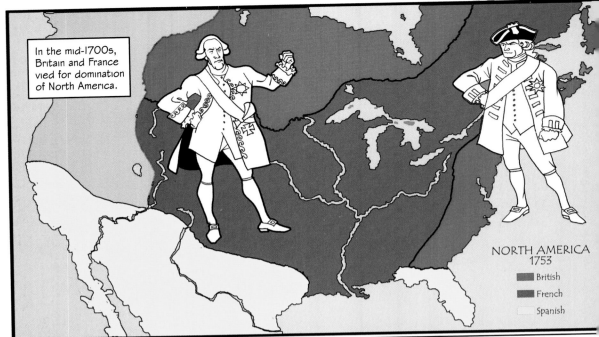

In the mid-1700s, Britain and France vied for domination of North America.

NORTH AMERICA
1753

■ British
■ French
□ Spanish

The center of contention was the fertile Ohio River Valley in what is now western Pennsylvania and Ohio. France longed for control of the Ohio River as a passageway linking New France with the Mississippi River. Britain wanted to extend its territory westward.

Ft. Laboef
Ft. Venango
ALLEGHENY R.
Pennsylvania
APPALACHIAN MTS.
OHIO R.
Ft. Duquesne
MONOGOHELA R.
Ft. Necessity
Virginia
Maryland

Campaign Routes
••••••• WASHINGTON 1754
●●●● BRADDOCK 1755
■ BRITISH FORT
□ FRENCH FORT
✳ BATTLE

Native Americans, longtime residents of the land claimed by the European powers, became alarmed when colonists began to settle on the western frontier. To protect their interests, tribes forged shifting alliances with the British and the French.

Twenty-two-year-old George Washington was sent to help build a British fort at the forks of the Ohio River. B the French got there first and built Fort Duquesne. As Washington deliberated over his next move, Half Kin a Mingo Indian ally, contacted hi

A FRENCH SCOUTING PARTY LIES NEARBY. SHOULD WE ATTACK THEM?

WE SHALL FALL ON THEM TOGETHER.

DON'T SHOOT, WE'LL YIELD.

I BEAR A MESSAGE FROM FORT DUQUESNE.

To prove his loyalty to the British, Half King killed the French ambassador. The French blamed Washington for the murder and vowed revenge on the British.

Fearing French retaliation, Washington and his men hastily built a stockade, which he grimly named *Fort Necessity*. When the French arrived, Washington's forces were outmanned and outgunned.

He surrendered after nine hours of slaughter.

He had lost the first battle of the French and Indian War.

Philadelphia, May 1754. Colonists knew that without British protection, settlers in the west would be attacked by the Indian allies of the French.

SET THIS EDITORIAL FOR TOMORROW'S EDITION: "THE ENGLISH COLONIES MUST FORM A STRONG UNION TO PROTECT OUR FRONTIERS. WE MUST JOIN OR DIE."

Albany, New York, July 1754. Representatives of seven colonies met to strengthen an alliance with the Iroquois Indians and discuss making a common defense against the French and *their* Indian allies. Benjamin Franklin attended as a delegate from Pennsylvania.

WASHINGTON HAS BEEN DEFEATED AT FORT NECESSITY. OUR FRONTIERS ARE IN PERIL!

DO YOU MEAN THE *PENNSYLVANIA* FRONTIER-- OR THE *VIRGINIA* FRONTIER . . . OR THE *NEW YORK* FRONTIER?

I REFER, SIR, TO *OUR* FRONTIER: READ MY *SHORT HINTS TOWARDS A SCHEME FOR UNITING THE NORTHERN COLONIES.*

WE WILL NOT PAY FOR NEW YORK FORTS.

WE MUST ALL UNITE TO DEFEND PENNSYLVANIA LAND IN THE WEST.

THE LAND YOU SPEAK OF BELONGS TO CONNECTICUT.

VIRGINIA LAYS CLAIM TO ALL THE TERRITORY WEST TO THE PACIFIC OCEAN.

WE BEG TO DIFFER!

Though they had many reasons to cooperate, the colonies continued to squabble over their competing interests.

Remarkably, the delegates finally accepted the Albany Plan of Union that Franklin submitted.

WE VOTE NAY!

NAY!

NAY!

But none of the *colonial legislatures* approved the plan. Each did not want to give up its independence from the other colonial legislatures and from Great Britain.

In the coming months, Indians attacked the frontiers, as Franklin and others had warned. Settlers came streaming back to the colonies.

Spring 1755. George Washington volunteered to guide British troops sent to attack Fort Duquesne. He offered advice to the British general Braddock, in charge of the assault.

IN THE WILDERNESS, RED COATS MAKE EASY TARGETS.

PSHAW! YOU COLONIALS KNOW NOTHING ABOUT WARFARE.

Washington found out what the British really thought of Americans . . .

. . . learned lessons about fighting in the woods . . .

. . . and witnessed a disastrous British defeat.

After nine years of fighting, Britain won--and removed the French from North America. For the moment, the British Empire had triumphed. But it would soon face an even greater challenge to its colonial rule.

Atlantic Ocean

AMERICA IN 1763
☐ 13 COLONIES
☐ BRITISH
☐ SPANISH

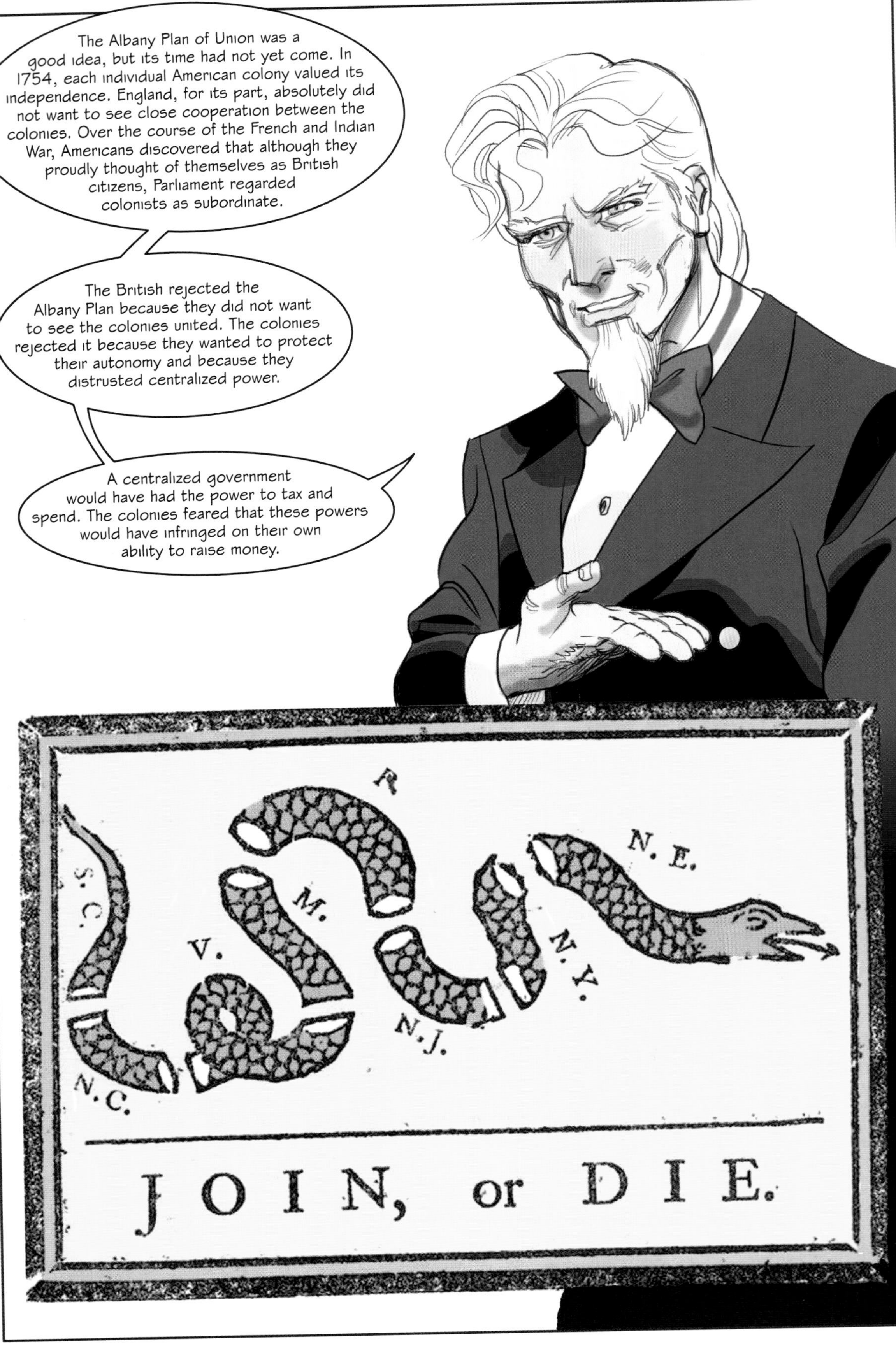
The Albany Plan of Union was a good idea, but its time had not yet come. In 1754, each individual American colony valued its independence. England, for its part, absolutely did not want to see close cooperation between the colonies. Over the course of the French and Indian War, Americans discovered that although they proudly thought of themselves as British citizens, Parliament regarded colonists as subordinate.
The British rejected the Albany Plan because they did not want to see the colonies united. The colonies rejected it because they wanted to protect their autonomy and because they distrusted centralized power.
A centralized government would have had the power to tax and spend. The colonies feared that these powers would have infringed on their own ability to raise money.
S.C.
N.C.
V.
M.
P.
N.J.
N.Y.
N.E.
JOIN, or DIE.

By 1765, American colonists had been mostly independent of direct British power for almost 150 years. They elected their own legislatures, passed their own local laws, and paid taxes for their own governments and militias. They were taxed by the British only indirectly. For instance, shippers and merchants paid taxes on imported goods.

Then, suddenly, the British decided to exert more direct control--and extract more money--and the colonies turned against their distant rulers.

Boston, August 14, 1765. The city erupted into protests when Great Britain attempted to tax the colonies without their consent.

THEY WANT TO PUT STAMPS ON EVERYTHING WE BUY! AND TAX THE STAMPS!

DOWN WITH THE STAMP TAX!

DEATH TO TAX COLLECTORS!

A.O. THE STAMP MAN

Expenses from the nine-year French and Indian War had left Britain with enormous bills, and 8,000 British soldiers had been left in North America to defend the frontier. They would have to be paid somehow.

AMERICANS SHOULD PAY FOR THEIR OWN DEFENSE!

Prime Minister George Grenville proposed a solution.

I AGREE, YOUR MAJESTY. I PROPOSE A STAMP TAX ON ALL COLONIAL DOCUMENTS.

DEBT

Grenville's stamp tax would apply to items used by merchants, lawyers, farmers, and sailors—ultimately, by every man and woman in the colonies.

House of Burgesses, Virginia, May 29, 1765. It took six weeks, by ship, for the news of the stamp tax to arrive. Then the colonies reacted. The young firebrand Patrick Henry was one of the first to protest the act.

Patrick Henry

SILENCE! SIT DOWN, SIR!

THE GENERAL ASSEMBLY OF THIS COLONY HAS THE *ONLY* RIGHT AND POWER TO LAY TAXES ON THE INHABITANTS . . .

Henry dared to compare George III to Julius Caesar and Charles I, who were both overthrown and killed by their enemies.

CAESAR HAD HIS BRUTUS; CHARLES I HAD HIS CROMWELL; AND GEORGE III . . .

. . . MAY PROFIT BY THEIR EXAMPLE. IF THIS BE TREASON, MAKE THE MOST OF IT!

TREASON! TREASON!

CAESAR

BRUTUS

CHARLES I

CROMWELL

Patrick Henry's Virginia Resolves were published in newspapers throughout the colonies. Fury over the Stamp Act exploded.

IF PARLIAMENT WANTS TO TAX VIRGINIA, IT MUST INCLUDE REPRESENTATIVES FROM VIRGINIA!

YES-- REPRESENTATIVES OF OUR OWN CHOOSING. OTHERWISE, WE'LL NOT USE THE STAMPS OR PAY THE TAX!

In Boston, mobs attacked the mansions of wealthy tax collectors and officeholders including the govenor, Thomas Hutchinson.

NO TAXATION WITHOUT REPRESENTATION!

Violent protests spread to other cities as well. Colonists everywhere were in agreement--the stamp tax had to go.

Newport, Rhode Island

New York City

Maryland

-31-

New York City, October 1765. Delegates from nine colonies met in what is known as the Stamp Act Congress. For the first time, the American colonies acted together to petition King George III and Parliament.

THE STAMP ACT DESTROYS THE RIGHTS AND LIBERTIES OF THE COLONISTS!

Parliament ignored the petitions. In protest, the colonists declared that *liberty was dead* and stopped buying British goods . . .

This is the Place to affix the STAMP.

Desperate British merchants begged Parliament to reconsider.

January 1766. Reluctantly, Parliament repealed the Stamp Act. Bells rang in celebration on both sides of the Atlantic.

Barely noticed was passage of another act declaring the absolute authority of the British government over the American colonies.

COLONISTS ARE BRITISH CITIZENS WITH *THE DUTIES* OF BRITISH CITIZENS, INCLUDING THE DUTY TO PAY TAXES.

COLONISTS ARE BRITISH CITIZENS WITH *THE RIGHTS* OF BRITISH CITIZENS, INCLUDING THE RIGHT NOT TO BE TAXED WITHOUT OUR CONSENT.

Future conflict seemed inevitable.

The Stamp Act crisis revealed basic disagreements between American colonists and Great Britain. Colonists maintained they could be taxed only by their duly elected representatives in colonial legislatures. Taxation *without* representation denied them their basic rights as British citizens. Parliament, for its part, insisted that it held total power over America, including the power to tax at will.

The crisis brought the colonies together in their first act of formal cooperation against the Crown. All colonists, from Maine to Georgia, viewed the Stamp Act as a threat to their liberty and vowed to defeat it.

EXCERPTS FROM THE VIRGINIA RESOLVES

"That the first adventurers and settlers of His Majesty's colony and dominion of Virginia brought with them . . . all the liberties . . . possessed by the people of Great Britain . . .

"That the taxation of the people by themselves, or by persons chosen by themselves to represent them . . . is the only security against a burdensome taxation, and the distinguishing characteristic of British freedom . . .

"Therefor that the General Assembly of this Colony have the only and exclusive Right and Power to lay Taxes and Impositions upon the inhabitants of this Colony and that every attempt to vest such Power in any person or persons whatsoever other than the General Assembly . . . has a manifest Tendency to destroy British as well as American Freedom."

After the repeal of the Stamp Act, colonists expected relations with Great Britain to improve. But they didn't. Instead, in 1767, Britain imposed another series of taxes, called the Townshend Acts. Colonists retaliated with boycotts, protests, and speeches. Again, the British were forced to back down.

Eventually, only one tax remained--*a tax on the importation of tea*, the colonists' favorite drink. In November 1773, three ships loaded with British tea entered Boston Harbor. On December 16, radical "Sons of Liberty" disguised as Mohawk Indians dumped 342 chests of tea into the harbor and ignited a crisis.

Within two years, colonists would be demanding independence from Great Britain, inspired by a revolutionary pamphlet called *Common Sense*.

House of Commons, London, April 1774. British reaction to the Boston Tea Party was swift.

THESE CRIMINALS HAVE DESTROYED VALUABLE PROPERTY!

BOSTON MUST BE PUNISHED.

WE MUST CONTROL THE COLONISTS.

Parliament passed a series of harsh laws called the Coercive Acts. Among other repressive measures, they closed the port of Boston and denied the people of Massachusetts the right to elect their own officials.

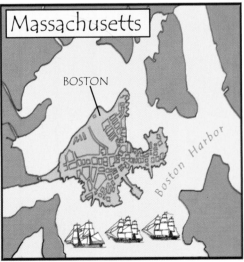

Massachusetts

BOSTON

Boston Harbor

British troops occupied Boston and closed the harbor. Much to Parliament's surprise, people from other colonies quickly came to the city's aid.

THIS FLOUR WILL HELP KEEP BOSTON FROM STARVING.

Outraged by the British response, delegates from all of the colonies except Georgia met in Philadelphia in September 1774 in the First Continental Congress. Radical members, such as Virginia's Patrick Henry, tried to unite all colonists in a common cause.

I AM NOT A VIRGINIAN BUT AN AMERICAN!

More conservative and moderate delegates like New York's John Jay stressed the long-standing ties between Britain and America.

WE *ARE* BRITISH CITIZENS AND CAN RELY ON THE *BRITISH CONSTITUTION* TO ASSERT OUR RIGHTS.

The Congress reached a historic agreement, deciding not to import or buy British goods. Also, each colony was urged to raise a militia for self-defense.

Lexington Common, April 19, 1775. When the British marched out of Boston to capture a colonial store of gunpowder, the Massachusetts militia, called Minutemen, were ready for them.

LAY DOWN YOUR ARMS!

No one knows who fired the first shot. But after a short volley, eight colonists were dead and ten others wounded. The Revolution had begun.

Philadelphia, May 10, 1775. Delegates to the Second Continental Congress were outraged about the carnage in Lexington, yet divided and uncertain of what to do.

THIS BLOODSHED SHOULD BE LAID AT THE FEET OF PARLIAMENT.

YES, HE IS!

LET US PETITION KING GEORGE HIMSELF TO RESTORE PEACE.

OUR KING IS NOT TO BLAME!

THE TIME FOR PEACE IS PAST! WE MUST *DEFEND* OURSELVES!

Loyalty to the king was still strong. John Dickinson of Pennsylvania persuaded the Congress to petition the king to reconcile.

To the king's most excellent Majesty:

Most Gracious Sovereign,

We, your Majesty's faithful subjects of the colonies of New Hampshire, Massachusetts Bay, Rhode island, Connecticut, New York, New Jersey, Pennsylvania, Delaware, Maryland, Virginia, North Carolina, South Carolina, and Georgia

However, John Adams of Massachusetts also convinced the delegates to appoint a general to lead the Continental army assembled to defend Boston.

I HAVE IN MIND A GENTLEMAN WHOSE SKILL AND EXPERIENCE AS AN OFFICER AND WHOSE EXCELLENT CHARACTER WOULD UNITE ALL THE COLONIES.

In the next months, the British and the Americans clashed often: in Boston, Maine, and Virginia. By the end of 1775, no one could deny that Britain and America were at war.

Yet the idea of independence remained unpopular. Many of those who had taken up arms still felt part of a loyal protest, not a revolution.

COMMON SENSE;

ADDRESSED TO THE

INHABITANTS

OF

AMERICA,

On the following interesting

SUBJECTS:

I. Of the Origin and Design of Government in general, with concise Remarks on the English Constitution.
II. Of Monarchy and Hereditary Succession.
III. Thoughts on the Present State of American Affairs.
IV. Of the present Ability of America, with some miscellaneous Reflections.

A NEW EDITION, with several Additions in the Body of the Work. To which is added, an APPENDIX; together with an Address to the People called QUAKERS.
N. B. The New Edition here given increases the Work upwards of One-Third.

By THOMAS PAINE,

Then a British immigrant named Thomas Paine wrote an electrifying pamphlet that changed the debate forever.

Only 46 pages long, *Common Sense* spoke directly to ordinary Americans.

"I offer nothing more than simple facts, plain arguments, and common sense."

Paine's mission was to convince colonists to make a complete break with Great Britain.

The time for independence had come.

"Now is the seed-time of continental union, faith, and honor."

AMERICAN PATRIOT

UNION FAITH HONOR LIBERTY

All monarchies are tyrannies, Paine asserted.

"For all men being originally equals, no one by birth could have a right to set up his own family in perpetual preference to all others forever."

And all monarchs are tyrants--even George III, whom Paine called the "royal brute."

"Of more worth is one honest man to society . . . than all the crowned ruffians that ever lived."

Americans do not owe the king or Great Britain their allegiance, he said.

DONT TREAD ON ME

"A government of our own is our natural right."

The cause of America is the cause of all mankind, Paine insisted.

Common Sense was published on January 10, 1776, and sold briskly. By the end of the year, Americans had bought 500,000 copies.

I AM FOR *COMMON SENSE* AND INDEPENDENCE!

AS AM I. WOULD YOU CARE FOR MORE LIBERTY TEA?

"This new world hath been the asylum for the persecuted lovers of civil and religious liberty from every part of Europe."

That same week, a newspaper published King George III's address to Parliament.

THE REBELS ARE NOW IN AN OPEN STATE OF REVOLT, HOSTILITY, AND REBELLION. BLOWS MUST DECIDE THE OUTCOME!

By refusing to accept Dickinson's Olive Branch Petition, the king proved that he was not interested in compromise.

In the spring of 1776, the idea of independence spread from city to town to village.

Americans everywhere understood and were moved by Paine's message: "We have it in our power to begin the world over again." The war for independence was soon at hand. The next fateful step was up to the Continental Congress.

Common Sense was perhaps the most influential publication in American history. It was read by men and women of all social ranks. It has been estimated that by the end of 1776, there was one copy for every five colonists.

Paine called for American independence when the idea was still controversial--and changed the minds of thousands.

He attacked the British monarchy directly, paving the way for Thomas Jefferson's condemnation of King George III in the Declaration of Independence.

Paine called for a republican government elected by the people. He said, "In America the law is king."

EXCERPTS FROM *COMMON SENSE*

"The sun never shined on a cause of greater worth. 'Tis not the affair of a city, a country, a province, or a kingdom, but of a continent . . . 'Tis not the concern of a day, a year, or an age; posterity are virtually involved in the contest, and will be more or less affected, even to the end of time, by the proceedings now. Now is the seed-time of continental union, faith, and honor . . .

"O ye that love mankind! Ye that dare oppose, not only the tyranny, but the tyrant, stand forth! Every spot of the old world is overrun with oppression. Freedom hath been hunted round the globe. Asia, and Africa, have long expelled her. Europe regards her like a stranger, and England hath given her warning to depart. O! receive the fugitive, and prepare in time an asylum for mankind."

The Declaration of Independence

Six long months passed between *Common Sense* and the Declaration of Independence. During that time, while Congress debated and armies clashed, Americans moved ever closer to a final break with Britain. When the right moment came, they were ready.

IT IS TRYING TO DESTROY OUR ECONOMY!

PARLIAMENT ITSELF IS PUSHING US TO INDEPENDENCE.

In winter 1775–76, events propelled the Second Continental Congress toward a decision, especially when colonists discovered that Parliament had blockaded all American trade and was attempting to confiscate American ships.

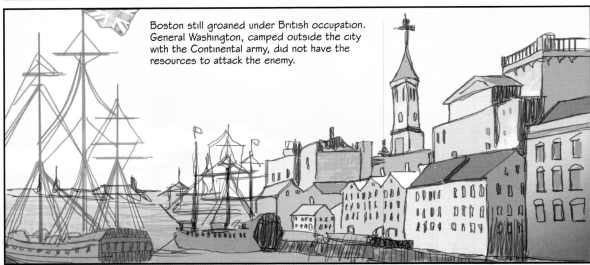

Boston still groaned under British occupation. General Washington, camped outside the city with the Continental army, did not have the resources to attack the enemy.

"TO THE CONGRESS: OUR SITUATION IS TRULY ALARMING. WE NEED MORE MEN AND GUNPOWDER IMMEDIATELY!"

Help arrived in mid-January. The American artillery captain Henry Knox hauled 59 cannon from Fort Ticonderoga in upstate New York all the way to Boston.

Washington had the firepower he needed. He decided to trap the British.

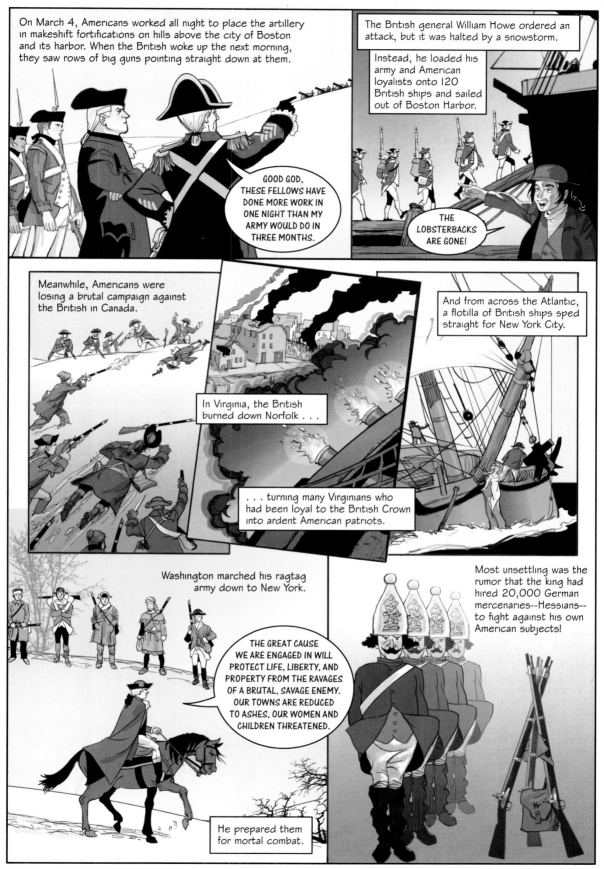

On March 4, Americans worked all night to place the artillery in makeshift fortifications on hills above the city of Boston and its harbor. When the British woke up the next morning, they saw rows of big guns pointing straight down at them.

GOOD GOD, THESE FELLOWS HAVE DONE MORE WORK IN ONE NIGHT THAN MY ARMY WOULD DO IN THREE MONTHS.

The British general William Howe ordered an attack, but it was halted by a snowstorm.

Instead, he loaded his army and American loyalists onto 120 British ships and sailed out of Boston Harbor.

THE LOBSTERBACKS ARE GONE!

Meanwhile, Americans were losing a brutal campaign against the British in Canada.

In Virginia, the British burned down Norfolk . . .

. . . turning many Virginians who had been loyal to the British Crown into ardent American patriots.

And from across the Atlantic, a flotilla of British ships sped straight for New York City.

Washington marched his ragtag army down to New York.

THE GREAT CAUSE WE ARE ENGAGED IN WILL PROTECT LIFE, LIBERTY, AND PROPERTY FROM THE RAVAGES OF A BRUTAL, SAVAGE ENEMY. OUR TOWNS ARE REDUCED TO ASHES, OUR WOMEN AND CHILDREN THREATENED.

He prepared them for mortal combat.

Most unsettling was the rumor that the king had hired 20,000 German mercenaries--Hessians-- to fight against his own American subjects!

Spring 1776. The Continental Congress told each colony to write a new constitution to replace its royal charter. In assemblies and town meetings, Americans started to vote for independence. They sent the results to their delegates in the Congress.

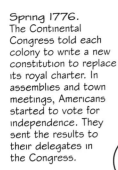

VIRGINIA

NORTH CAROLINA

RHODE ISLAND

WE SHALL IMMEDIATELY CAST OFF THE BRITISH YOKE.

WE SHALL JOIN WITH OTHER COLONIES IN DECLARING INDEPENDENCE.

WE SHALL NO LONGER SWEAR OUR OATH OF ALLEGIANCE TO THE KING!

Massachusetts delegate John Adams, who led the independence movement in Congress, wrote to a friend in great excitement.

EVERY POST AND EVERY DAY ROLLS IN UPON US, INDEPENDENCE LIKE A TORRENT.

Yet some delegates--especially in the Middle Colonies of New York, New Jersey, and Pennsylvania--were not ready for independence. Many of their citizens were Loyalists, businessmen, and government officials, reluctant or unwilling to make the final break from Britain and the king.

LET US NOT BE HASTY!

In the meantime, the American invasion of Canada was heading for disaster. While in New York City, Washington anxiously scanned the horizon for the enemy armada. The Congress debated what to do.

State House, Pennsylvania, June 7. Richard Henry Lee of Virginia stood up in the Congress and presented a resolution approved by his legislature:

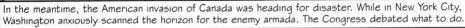
WE MUST SEE IF THE FRENCH COURT WILL ALLY WITH US AGAINST THE MIGHT OF THE BRITISH.

I PROPOSE A RESOLUTION!

"These United Colonies are, and of rights ought to be, free and independent States; that they are absolved from all allegiance to the British Crown; and that all political connection between them and the state of Great Britain is, and ought to be, totally dissolved."

A vigorous debate began. The Pennsylvania delegate John Dickinson, speaking for the moderates, argued fervently against the resolution.

SOME COLONIES HAVE NOT VOTED FOR INDEPENDENCE.

WE DON'T NEED TO BE INDEPENDENT TO WIN THE WAR.

RECONCILIATION WITH THE MOTHER COUNTRY WOULD BE BEST FOR THE THIRTEEN COLONIES.

John Adams spoke for the radicals.

DECLARING INDEPENDENCE JUST CONFIRMS WHAT HAS ALREADY HAPPENED.

MOST AMERICANS WANT INDEPENDENCE!

Seven delegations supported the resolution for independence. Six--those of Pennsylvania, New York, New Jersey, Maryland, Delaware, and South Carolina--did not.

On June 10, Edward Rutledge of South Carolina moved to postpone a final vote for three weeks. The delay provided the Congress the time to write a formal declaration of independence. The Congress appointed a committee to accomplish this task:

Benjamin Franklin
Pennsylvania
Writer, statesman, and inventor

Thomas Jefferson
Virginia
Brilliant young lawyer

Robert Livingston
New York
Wealthy moderate

Roger Sherman
Connecticut
Plainspoken lawyer

John Adams
Massachusetts
Outspoken radical

But who would write the first draft of the declaration? The committee quickly came to a conclusion.

I AM TOO UNPOPULAR.

THE WRITER SHOULD BE A SOUTHERNER, NOT A NORTHERNER.

MR. JEFFERSON, YOU ARE THE BEST WRITER AMONG US.

The committee agreed on the basic form and content of the document, then Jefferson drafted it. He wanted to express what most Americans were thinking--to capture the "tone and spirit" of "the American mind."

He drew upon the philosophical ideas of European thinkers like John Locke and on colonial declarations of independence--especially Virginia's Declaration of Rights.

Jefferson divided the declaration into three sections: the introduction; the list of wrongs perpetrated by the king; and the conclusion.

The first paragraph of the introduction states that the time has come for Americans to cut their ties with Great Britain . . .

. . . and take their place among all the self-governing peoples of the world.

NOW WE ARE PROCLAIMING OUR INDEPENDENCE!

We hold these truths to be self-evident

The second paragraph of the declaration expresses the fundamental principles of the new nation: that "all men are created equal" and have natural rights that cannot be taken away from them.

By equality, Jefferson actually did not mean that everyone has the same *abilities*. Rather, he suggests that all human beings are born with the same God-given and legal *rights*.

EQUAL RIGHTS

Yet in 18th-century America, all individuals did not have the same rights under the law. White men who did not own land or buildings, as well as all women, Indians, and slaves, did not have the same privileges as white men with property. Since that time, Jefferson's idea of equality has remained an *ideal*, a goal toward which we still strive.

The declaration defined natural human rights as including those of "life, liberty, and the pursuit of Happiness" and said that governments are founded to protect these rights.

Life

Liberty

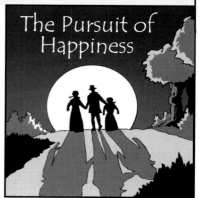

The Pursuit of Happiness

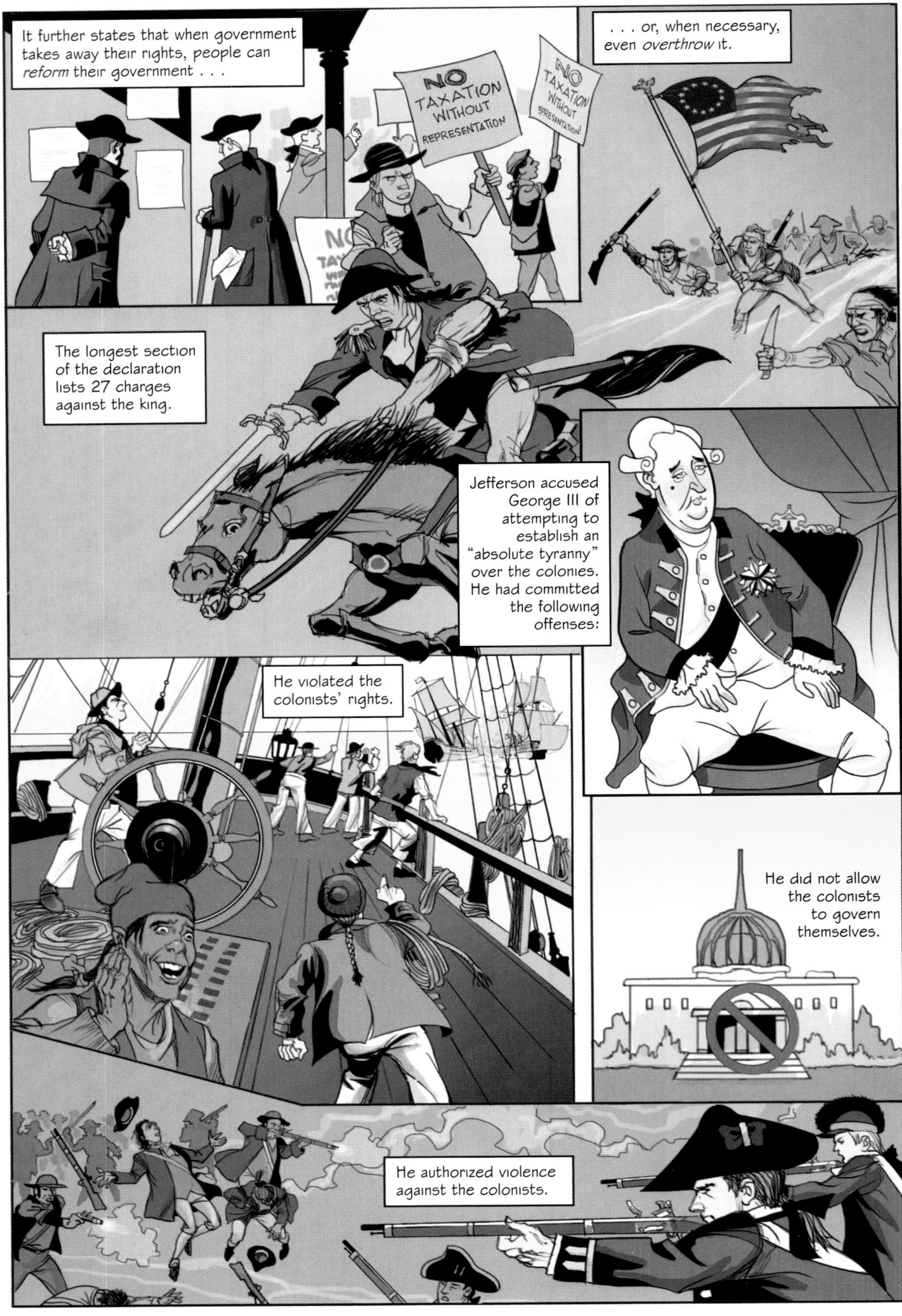
It further states that when government takes away their rights, people can *reform* their government . . .
NO TAXATION WITHOUT REPRESENTATION
NO TAXATION WITHOUT REPRESENTATION!
. . . or, when necessary, even *overthrow* it.
The longest section of the declaration lists 27 charges against the king.
Jefferson accused George III of attempting to establish an "absolute tyranny" over the colonies. He had committed the following offenses:
He violated the colonists' rights.
He did not allow the colonists to govern themselves.
He authorized violence against the colonists.

We therefore the representatives of the United States of america, in general congress, assembled appealing to the supreme Judge of the world for the rectitude of our intentions, do, in the name, and by the authority of the good people of these colonies, solemnly publish and declare, that these united colonies are, and of right ought to be free and independent states.

While Jefferson wrote, the British routed the American forces in Canada.

And a huge fleet of British warships sailed into New York Harbor.

On June 28, the committee formally presented the Declaration of Independence to the Second Continental Congress.

WE NEED THE PROTECTION OF GREAT BRITAIN!

On July 1, the delegates once again took up Richard Henry Lee's resolution of independence. And the debate went on.

The door banged open, and five new delegates from New Jersey marched in--and they voted for independence.

EITHER WE DECLARE AMERICAN INDEPENDENCE, OR WE REMAIN FOREVER SUBORDINATE!

Each colony cast one preliminary vote on the resolution. The final ballot would be taken the next day. At first, nine states voted yes.

NH MA RI CT NJ MD VA NC GA

Two states voted no.

PA   SC

One state abstained.

NY

And one state was divided.

DE

That night, the ailing Delaware delegate Caesar Rodney rode 80 miles from his home to Philadelphia to cast his vote for independence.

After independence had been declared, the Congress spent two days honing Jefferson's draft.

JULY 2, 1776. In the final vote, South Carolina and Delaware ratified independence. So did Pennsylvania. Only New York abstained--its delegates had never received instructions from their legislature. Two weeks later, they were able to vote for ratification.

On July 4, the declaration was approved. All knew that this would be seen as an act of treason against Great Britain. They pledged to one another "our lives, our Fortunes, and our sacred Honor."

WE MUST BE UNANIMOUS.

WE MUST ALL HANG TOGETHER. OR MOST ASSUREDLY, WE SHALL ALL HANG SEPARATELY.

John Hancock, president of the Second Continental Congress, signed the declaration the same day. The other delegates waited until the document could be copied onto fine parchment paper, which they all signed.

New York City, July 9. Washington ordered the Declaration of Independence read to the troops.

Afterward, an enthusiastic crowd pulled down a lead statue of King George. The metal was melted down for bullets.

An ecstatic John Adams wrote home to his wife, Abigail:

THE SECOND DAY OF JULY WILL BE CELEBRATED BY SUCCEEDING GENERATIONS, AS THE GREAT ANNIVERSARY FESTIVAL . . . WITH POMP AND PARADE, WITH SHOWS, GAMES, SPORTS, GUNS, BELLS, BONFIRES, AND ILLUMINATIONS.

Americans do celebrate Independence Day, but on July 4, the day the Declaration of Independence was approved.

The opening sentence announces that the American people are one unified body, not citizens of separate royal colonies, and that they are proclaiming their right to form their own government.

The document explains to the world why it was necessary for Americans to split from Great Britain.

In the second paragraph, Jefferson sums up philosophical ideas about inherent human rights. The English philosopher John Locke named these rights "life, liberty, and estate [property]." Jefferson changed "estate" to "pursuit of happiness," emphasizing the individualism that has marked Americans ever since.

He also wrote that "all men are created equal." These were inspiring words, though even in Jefferson's day they did not truly describe the condition of all people in the colonies.

People agree to form governments to protect these rights. When governments fail to do so, people have the right to revolt and form new governments. The list of grievances that follows details the ways in which the king of Great Britain failed to protect the "Life, Liberty and the pursuit of Happiness" of the American people. Jefferson lists these grievances to prove to the world that the American Revolution is justified.

EXCERPTS FROM
THE DECLARATION OF INDEPENDENCE

"When in the Course of human events, it becomes necessary for one people to dissolve the political bands which have connected them with another, and to assume among the powers of the earth, the separate and equal station to which the Laws of Nature and of Nature's God entitle them, a decent respect to the opinions of mankind requires that they should declare the causes which impel them to the separation.

"We hold these truths to be self-evident, that all men are created equal, that they are endowed by their Creator with certain unalienable Rights, that among these are Life, Liberty and the pursuit of Happiness.--That to secure these rights, Governments are instituted among Men, deriving their just powers from the consent of the governed.--That whenever any Form of Government becomes destructive of these ends, it is the Right of the People to alter or to abolish it, and to institute new Government, laying its foundation on such principles and organizing its powers in such form, as to them shall seem most likely to effect their Safety and Happiness."

The conclusion officially names "the united States of America." The uppercase word "States" emphasizes that the individual states remain separate from one another and powerful in their own right, even though they have joined together.

It formally declares the new nation's independence from Great Britain.

This nation claims all the powers of an independent country--the ability to wage war, make alliances, and conduct trade.

"We, therefore, the Representatives of the united States of America, in General Congress, Assembled, appealing to the Supreme Judge of the world for the rectitude of our intentions, do, in the Name, and by Authority of the good People of these Colonies, solemnly publish and declare, That these United Colonies are, and of Right ought to be Free and Independent States; that they are Absolved from all Allegiance to the British Crown, and that all political connection between them and the State of Great Britain, is and ought to be totally dissolved; and that as Free and Independent States, they have full Power to levy War, conclude Peace, contract Alliances, establish Commerce, and to do all other Acts and Things which Independent States may of right do. And for the support of this Declaration, with a firm reliance on the protection of divine Providence, we mutually pledge to each other our Lives, our Fortunes and our sacred Honor."

The Crisis

Just five months after the nation declared its independence, General Washington's Continental army seemed on the edge of collapse. In the darkest hour of the American Revolution, Thomas Paine once again wrote a pamphlet--*The American Crisis*--that aroused the patriotism of the American people and helped propel the army to victory.

Brooklyn, New York, 1776. Washington's string of defeats had begun in August, at the Battle of Long Island. His troops were forced to retreat across the East River to New York City . . .

. . . and then the British chased them up Manhattan Island and across New Jersey.

Delaware River, December 25, 1776. But Paine's inspirational words helped strengthen the resolve of the American soldiers. Washington planned a daring move. In the dead of night, he transported his army across an ice-choked river to surprise an unprepared enemy.

Washington knew full well that the next 24 hours could bring triumph--or ruin.

December 8, 1776. Crossing into Pennsylvania, the army huddled in the snow on the west banks of the Delaware River, enemy troops on the opposite shore. Washington's men were freezing, sick, ragged, and discouraged.

THOSE BRITISH THIEVES STOLE ALL MY CATTLE AND MY BEST FEATHER BED!

Most planned to go home as soon as their term of enlistment was up at the end of the month.

Thomas Paine, working as a war correspondent, retreated with the rest of the army across British-occupied New Jersey. He observed the suffering of civilians . . .

Paine walked the 35 miles to Philadelphia to finish his manuscript and find a printer.

. . . and the gloom of the enlisted troops.

He decided to send a patriotic message to revive the revolutionary cause.

PRINT 18,000 COPIES IMMEDIATELY!

A week before Christmas, *The American Crisis* was published. Within days, it was circulating among civilians and soldiers alike, stirring, as Paine had hoped, the spirit of independence.

Washington seized the moment to plot a sneak attack on German Hessian troops camped across the river at Trenton, New Jersey. Before his 2,400 troops set off, their officers read them *The Crisis*.

"These are the times that try men's souls . . ."

Then, in the dead of night, Washington moved his army across the river.

By 4 a.m., all 2,400 men had crossed the Delaware and landed in New Jersey.

They trudged toward Trenton . . .

PRESS ON, PRESS ON!

. . . and caught the Hessians totally by surprise. Washington's triumph was complete.

A few days later, he won another startling victory against the British at Princeton. The war for independence would last another four years. But in this week, General Washington's army--with the help of Thomas Paine--won the confidence of the American people.

EXCERPTS FROM *THE CRISIS*

"These are the times that try men's souls. The summer soldier and the sunshine patriot will, in this crisis, shrink from the service of their country; but he that stands it now, deserves the love and thanks of man and woman."

"Tyranny, like hell, is not easily conquered; yet we have this consolation with us, that the harder the conflict, the more glorious the triumph. What we obtain too cheap, we esteem too lightly: it is dearness only that gives everything its value."

The Constitution

The American Revolution lasted seven long years after the signing of the Declaration of Independence. During this time the Continental Congress united the states under a constitution called the Articles of Confederation. After the American victory against the British, the Articles remained the law of the land. Yet it soon became apparent that a stronger, more cohesive government was needed. Once again, delegates gathered in Philadelphia to decide the future of the country. Together they forged the Constitution of the United States.

Against enormous odds, George Washington and the Continental army--with the crucial help of their French allies--had won the Battle of Yorktown in 1781, signaling the end of the Revolutionary War. Some fighting continued until the war was officially concluded with the Paris Peace Treaty, signed in 1783.

Great Britain recognized the United States as an independent nation and fixed its borders at the Atlantic Ocean in the east and the Mississippi River in the west.

Yorktown, Virginia, 1781.

After the British surrendered, some Continental army officers wanted to make Washington king of America.

I FOUGHT FOR A REPUBLIC, NOT A MONARCHY!

IF HE RESIGNS, WASHINGTON WILL BE THE GREATEST MAN IN THE WORLD.

Instead, Washington ignored them and resigned from the army, retiring to his estate in Virginia. King George was amazed that he would voluntarily give up power.

Canada
BRITISH COLONIES

United States

Louisiana
SPANISH COLONIES

NORTH AMERICA
1783

Washington had a vision of the "Citizens of America" as the sole "Lords and Proprietors" of a "vast Tract of Continent" and "possessed of absolute freedom and Independency."

Yet most Americans--even the Founding Fathers--still thought of themselves first and foremost as citizens of their home states, not the United States.

VIRGINIA IS MY COUNTRY.

MASSACHUSETTS IS MY COUNTRY.

Americans felt they had revolted in order to rid themselves of a powerful central government. So when the Congress wrote the Articles of Confederation in 1777, it created a deliberately weak central government--with no king or president.

NY MA RI NH CT NJ DE PA VA MD NC SC GA

The Articles formed a "firm league of friendship" among equal, sovereign states.

Under the Articles, the Confederation Congress was able to:

1. Declare war ✓
2. Raise an army ✓
3. Negotiate treaties ✓
4. Collect taxes ✗
5. Regulate trade ✗

Unfortunately, the United States had emerged from the war with enormous debts. The nation had to pay its creditors--but the states did not want to give the Congress the money.

European powers saw that the new nation was weak and disorganized . . . and refused to honor the terms of the Treaty of Paris.

HONOR OUR PEACE TREATY! CLOSE THIS FORT!

YOU CANNOT FORCE ME!

British fort in Ohio River Valley

The states squabbled among themselves--about territory, taxes, and trade. When the value of the American dollar dropped, each state printed its own money.

By 1784, the United States had sunk into an economic depression.

THIS IS NORTH CAROLINA. WE DO NOT ACCEPT GEORGIA DOLLARS HERE!

Massachusetts, 1786.

Farmers in Massachusetts were hit especially hard. They could not pay their state's high taxes.

THE STATE HAS SEIZED MY FARM BECAUSE I OWE BACK TAXES.

WE WILL FIGHT BACK AND PROTECT OUR PROPERTY!

A farmer named Daniel Shays organized an armed militia. They stormed across the state, attacking tax collectors and destroying courthouses.

Since the Congress could not raise money from the states to fight the rebels, rich Massachusetts citizens hired a *private army*.

Shays's Rebellion was suppressed--but protests also occurred in other states.

George Washington was dismayed by the unrest and by the weakness of the Congress. He and James Madison, a brilliant, bookish young Virginian, discussed a plan of action.

WE MUST FORM A NEW, STRONGER GOVERNMENT.

LET US CALL FOR A GRAND CONVENTION OF THE STATES TO REVISE THE ARTICLES OF CONFEDERATION.

Philadelphia, May 1787.

Other reform leaders agreed. In spring 1787, delegates from 12 states gathered at the Pennsylvania State House to work out a plan of government. Rhode Island was the only state that did not attend.

Eventually, the framers of the Constitution would number 55; Thomas Jefferson would later call them an "assembly of demi-gods." Jefferson himself was not present in Philadelphia, however--he and John Adams were serving as U.S. ambassadors in Europe.

Benjamin Franklin

George Washington

Alexander Hamilton

James Madison

The first order of business was to elect a president of the convention.

I NOMINATE GEORGE WASHINGTON!

During the convention, Washington made only one speech. Yet his leadership held all the delegates together.

The delegates took an oath to work in absolute secrecy so that they could speak freely. The windows were nailed shut, the doors were closed, and guards turned away all visitors.

James Madison later commented, "No Constitution would ever have been adopted by the public if the debates had been public."

PA

MA

VA

Large

Confidentiality was a good idea because the states were not united. Sharp divisions would arise between the largest and the smallest states . . .

NJ

MD

Small

DE

CT

Northern

MA

CT

Southern

MD

GA

. . . and between the Northern and the Southern states.

PA

NY

NC

SC

VA

-59-

May 29, 1787.

VIRGINIA PLAN

Edmund Randolph, governor of Virginia, rose to present a plan that Madison and others had hammered out. The Virginia Plan would form the basis for debates for the next three months.

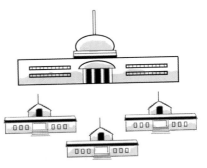

The plan overthrew the Articles of Confederation. Instead of a weak central government and strong states, it proposed a strong central government and states with more limited but still important powers.

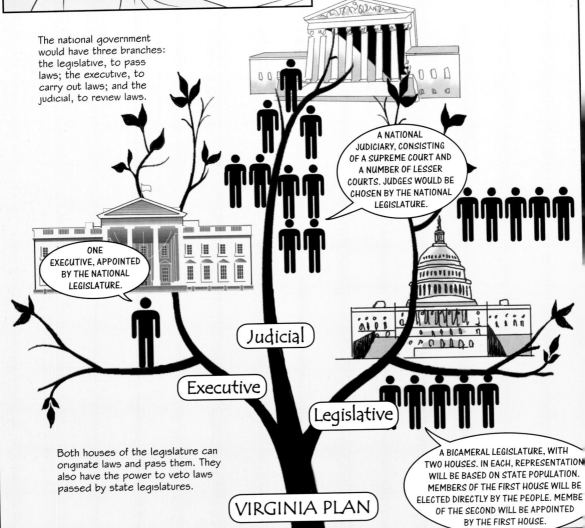

The national government would have three branches: the legislative, to pass laws; the executive, to carry out laws; and the judicial, to review laws.

A NATIONAL JUDICIARY, CONSISTING OF A SUPREME COURT AND A NUMBER OF LESSER COURTS. JUDGES WOULD BE CHOSEN BY THE NATIONAL LEGISLATURE.

ONE EXECUTIVE, APPOINTED BY THE NATIONAL LEGISLATURE.

Judicial

Executive

Legislative

Both houses of the legislature can originate laws and pass them. They also have the power to veto laws passed by state legislatures.

A BICAMERAL LEGISLATURE, WITH TWO HOUSES. IN EACH, REPRESENTATION WILL BE BASED ON STATE POPULATION. MEMBERS OF THE FIRST HOUSE WILL BE ELECTED DIRECTLY BY THE PEOPLE. MEMBE OF THE SECOND WILL BE APPOINTED BY THE FIRST HOUSE.

VIRGINIA PLAN

I SAID FIX IT UP, NOT KNOCK IT DOWN!

ARTICLES

The far-reaching plan sparked immediate controversy. Most delegates had not come to overturn the Articles of Confederation--merely to revise them. For many, the proposed changes were too radical.

Under the Articles, ALL representatives to Congress were chosen by their state legislatures. In the Virginia Plan, at least some would be elected directly by the people, a prospect that alarmed many delegates.

PEOPLE ARE LESS FIT JUDGES.

AN ENERGETIC GOVERNMENT WILL FLOW IMMEDIATELY FROM THE *PEOPLE*.

ELECTION BY THE *PEOPLE* IS ESSENTIAL TO FREE GOVERNMENT.

THE *PEOPLE* ARE LIABLE TO BE MISLED.

But the most contentious question of proportional representation remained. Small states were frantic that they would lose all their power to the large states.

IN THE NATIONAL LEGISLATURE, VIRGINIA WILL HAVE 16 VOTES, AND GEORGIA ONLY 1!

I DECLARE THAT I WILL NEVER CONSENT TO THIS UNFAIR SYSTEM!

June 15, 1787. The New Jersey Plan.

NEW JERSEY PLAN

Virginia Plan

Representatives of the "small states" submitted their own preferred plan for government. The New Jersey Plan revised the Articles of Confederation, enlarging the power of the central government. All states, large or small, had equal votes in the legislature.

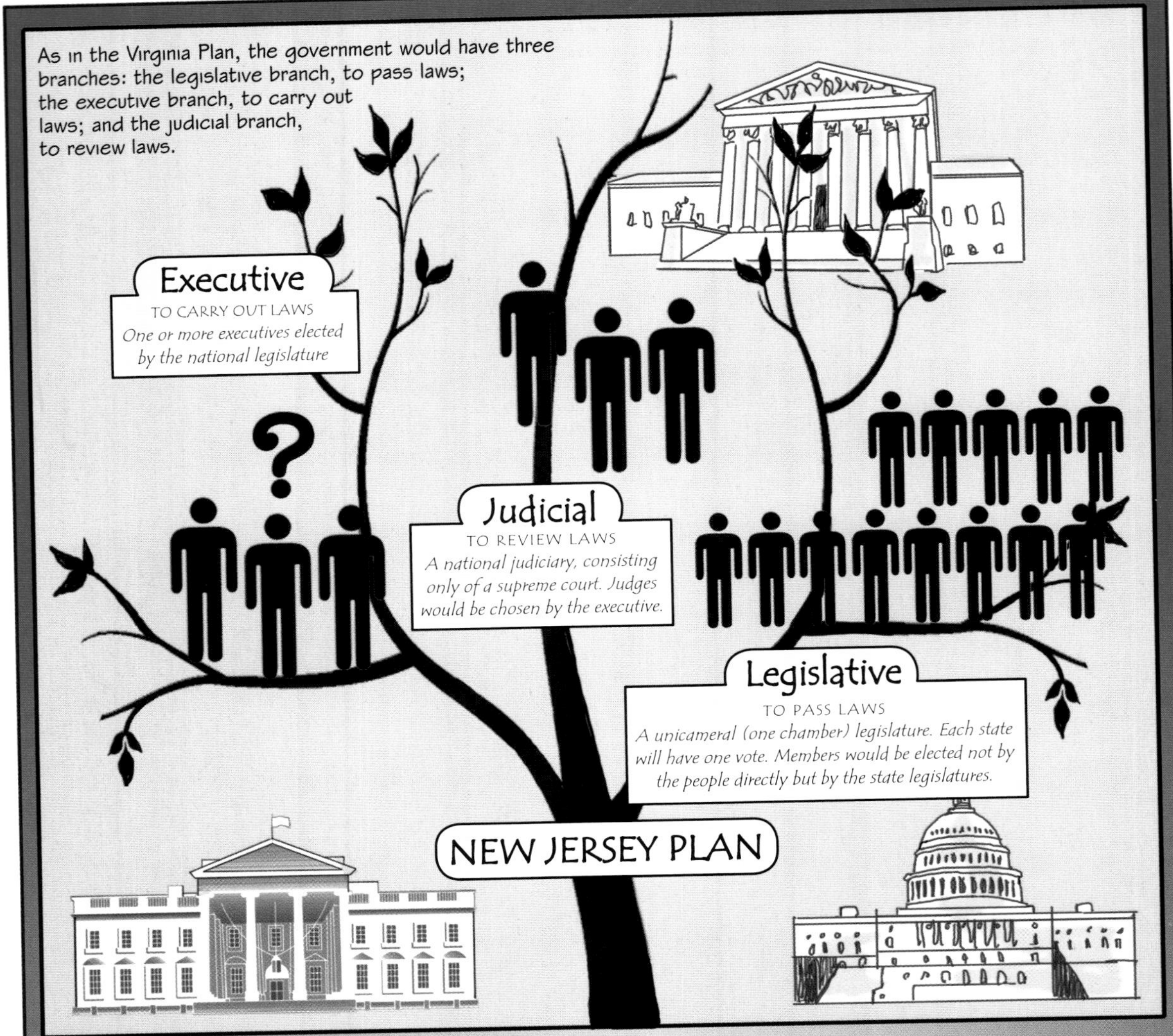
As in the Virginia Plan, the government would have three branches: the legislative branch, to pass laws; the executive branch, to carry out laws; and the judicial branch, to review laws.
Executive
TO CARRY OUT LAWS
One or more executives elected by the national legislature
Judicial
TO REVIEW LAWS
A national judiciary, consisting only of a supreme court. Judges would be chosen by the executive.
Legislative
TO PASS LAWS
A unicameral (one chamber) legislature. Each state will have one vote. Members would be elected not by the people directly but by the state legislatures.
NEW JERSEY PLAN

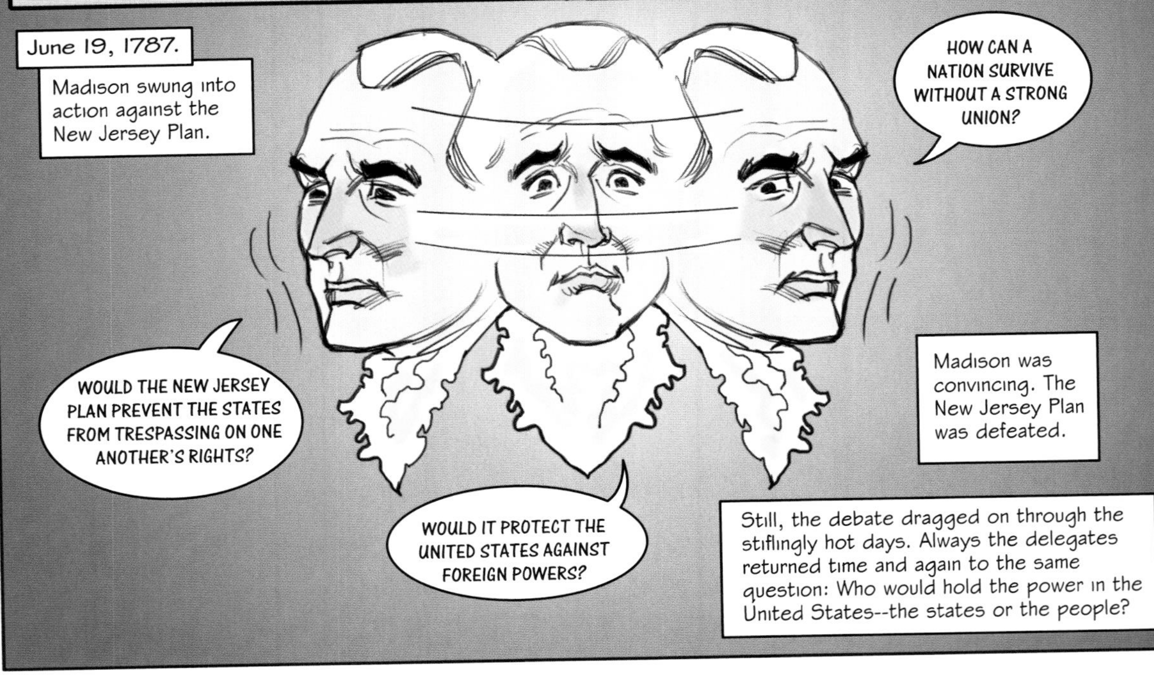
June 19, 1787.
Madison swung into action against the New Jersey Plan.
HOW CAN A NATION SURVIVE WITHOUT A STRONG UNION?
WOULD THE NEW JERSEY PLAN PREVENT THE STATES FROM TRESPASSING ON ONE ANOTHER'S RIGHTS?
WOULD IT PROTECT THE UNITED STATES AGAINST FOREIGN POWERS?
Madison was convincing. The New Jersey Plan was defeated.
Still, the debate dragged on through the stiflingly hot days. Always the delegates returned time and again to the same question: Who would hold the power in the United States--the states or the people?

During the debates, emotions ran high, and a solution seemed impossible.

LARGE STATES

THE LARGE STATES WILL CRUSH THE SMALL ONES. I DO NOT, GENTLEMEN, TRUST YOU!

Eighty-one-year-old Benjamin Franklin tried to calm everyone down. Perhaps they should pray for divine guidance, he said. The future was at stake.

IF WE ARE DEFEATED, MANKIND MAY DESPAIR OF EVER FORMING A GOVERNMENT BY HUMAN WISDOM.

All delegates were aware that the rest of the world--and the fate of future generations-- awaited their actions. It was crucial that they not fail.

Even Washington was deeply discouraged.

THE CRISIS IS EQUALLY IMPORTANT AND ALARMING . . . I ALMOST DESPAIR OF SEEING A FAVORABLE ISSUE TO THE PROCEEDINGS OF THE CONVENTION.

The convention had reached a stalemate. In desperation, the delegates turned to a compromise first introduced by Roger Sherman--a successful lawyer and Connecticut politician.

Sherman suggested that all states, no matter their size, have two senators in the Senate. This idea satisfied the smaller states. However, the number of members in the House of Representatives would be based on state population. This plan pleased the larger states.

Under Sherman's plan, for instance, in 1790, congressional representation for Virginia, Connecticut, and Delaware would look like this:

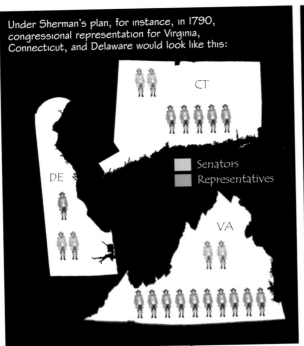

CT

DE

■ Senators
■ Representatives

VA

July 16. This agreement, known as the Great Compromise, saved the Constitutional Convention. Although some large-state delegates objected, the compromise passed by one vote. The delegates, energized by the success, went on to resolve other big issues . . .

. . . such as the role and power of the chief executive. These former revolutionaries distrusted concentrated power in any one individual's hands. Yet an effective government would require an authoritative executive branch to counterbalance the power of the legislature. How many executives would there be?

ONE MAN

THREE MEN

And how long would one or all three executives serve?

ONE-YEAR TERM

FIFTEEN-YEAR TERM

LIFE TERM

Eventually, the framers decided that there would be one president and that he would hold office long enough to be effective.

FOUR-YEAR TERM

Outside the State House, rumors began swirling that the delegates were setting up a monarchy. Perhaps they would invite George III's son to be king! Washington put out the word: "Though we cannot tell you what we are doing, we have never once thought of a king."

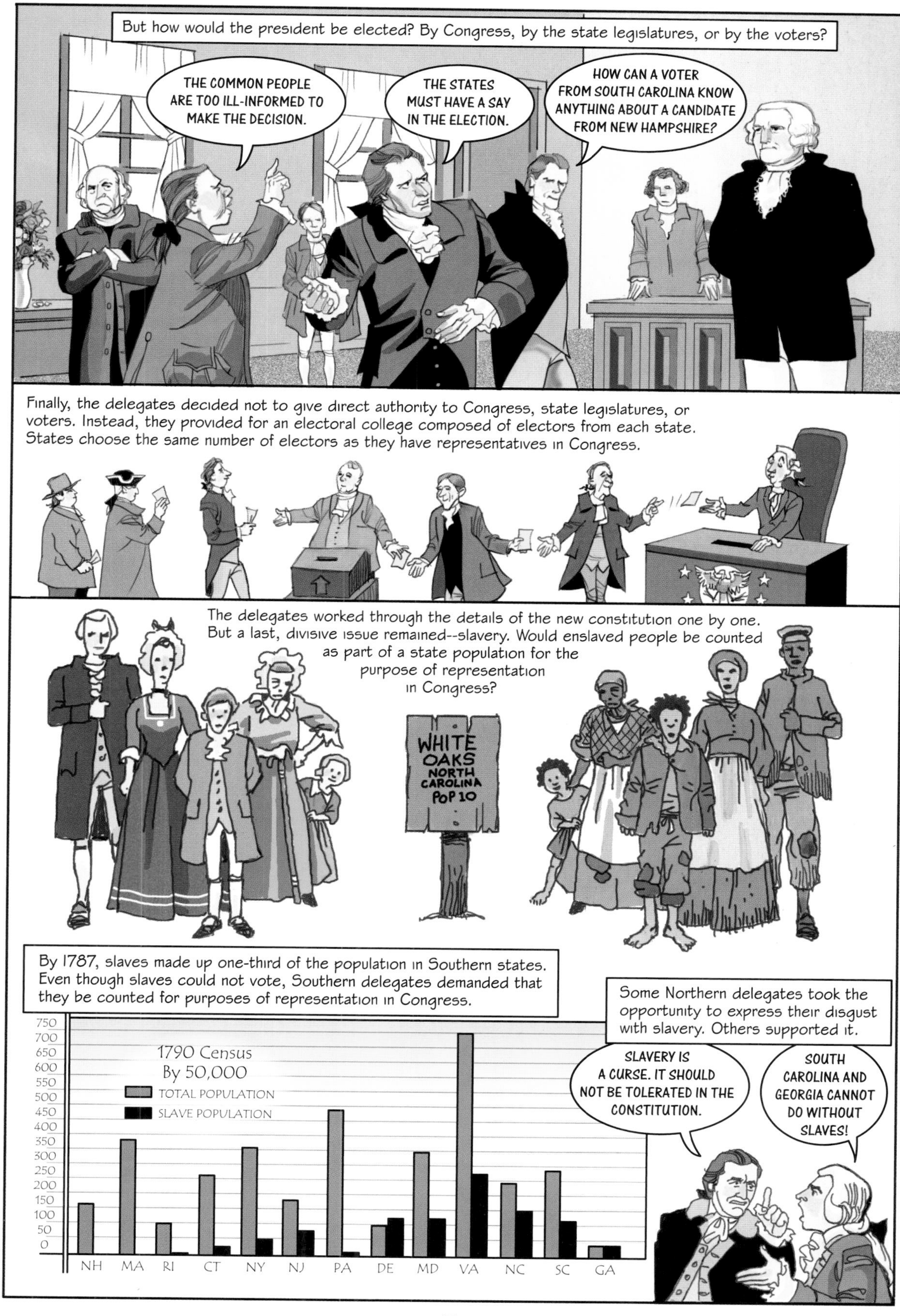
But how would the president be elected? By Congress, by the state legislatures, or by the voters?
THE COMMON PEOPLE ARE TOO ILL-INFORMED TO MAKE THE DECISION.
THE STATES MUST HAVE A SAY IN THE ELECTION.
HOW CAN A VOTER FROM SOUTH CAROLINA KNOW ANYTHING ABOUT A CANDIDATE FROM NEW HAMPSHIRE?
Finally, the delegates decided not to give direct authority to Congress, state legislatures, or voters. Instead, they provided for an electoral college composed of electors from each state. States choose the same number of electors as they have representatives in Congress.
The delegates worked through the details of the new constitution one by one. But a last, divisive issue remained--slavery. Would enslaved people be counted as part of a state population for the purpose of representation in Congress?
WHITE OAKS NORTH CAROLINA POP 10
By 1787, slaves made up one-third of the population in Southern states. Even though slaves could not vote, Southern delegates demanded that they be counted for purposes of representation in Congress.
1790 Census
By 50,000
TOTAL POPULATION
SLAVE POPULATION
750
700
650
600
550
500
450
400
350
300
250
200
150
100
50
0
NH
MA
RI
CT
NY
NJ
PA
DE
MD
VA
NC
SC
GA
Some Northern delegates took the opportunity to express their disgust with slavery. Others supported it.
SLAVERY IS A CURSE. IT SHOULD NOT BE TOLERATED IN THE CONSTITUTION.
SOUTH CAROLINA AND GEORGIA CANNOT DO WITHOUT SLAVES!

Even those who opposed slavery knew that some delegates would not agree to abolish it within the United States. Yet in the new constitution, Congress was given the power to regulate trade. Could the Constitution abolish the slave trade?

IT IS AN INFERNAL TRAFFIC!

THE TRUE QUESTION AT PRESENT IS WHETHER THE SOUTHERN STATES SHALL EVEN REMAIN IN THE UNION!

VA

IT IS BETTER TO LET SOUTHERN STATES IMPORT SLAVES THAN TO PART WITH THESE STATES.

CT

SC

Rather than lose the Southern states, the delegates reached a compromise. The Three-Fifths Compromise provided that each slave would be counted as three-fifths of a person in a state's population count.*

WHITE OAKS NORTH CAROLINA POP 10

In return, the Constitution would state that Congress could prohibit the slave trade in 20 years.

Compromise left the problem of slavery up to future generations. But without compromise, the Constitution would not have been completed or ratified.

*In 1863, the 13th Amendment outlawed slavery, invalidating the Three-Fifths Compromise. The 15th Amendment gave black men the vote.

The foundation of the new constitution was built on compromise and balance. From the beginning, the delegates had wrestled with the question of how to share power--between the government and the people, the national government and the states, the big states and the small states, and the North and the South.

The division of power between the national government and the states is called *federalism*. The framers of the Constitution worked out a system whereby some powers belong to the states and some to the national government.

For instance, the national government has the power to:

Regulate interstate and foreign trade	Coin money	Declare war	Raise an army and a navy	Pass all laws needed to carry out its powers

The states have the power to:

Establish schools	Conduct elections	Establish local governments	Regulate trade within the state	Do anything not forbidden to the states or granted to the national government

National and state governments *both* have the power to:

Collect taxes	Borrow money	Establish courts	Enforce laws	Build roads

The Constitution also establishes a separation of powers within the federal government itself. The framers borrowed the idea from the French philosopher Montesquieu, who recommended three branches of government to prevent tyranny.

President

I CAN PROPOSE LAWS → BUT I MIGHT NOT PASS THEM → AND I CAN DECLARE THEM UNCONSTITUTIONAL

I CAN MAKE TREATIES → BUT I HAVE TO RATIFY THEM → AND I CAN DECLARE EXECUTIVE ACTIONS UNCONSTITUTIONAL

I CAN MAKE APPOINTMENTS → BUT I MUST CONFIRM THEM

I POSSESS GREAT POWER → BUT I CAN IMPEACH AND REMOVE YOU

President

Congress   Courts

I CAN PASS LAWS → BUT I CAN VETO THEM → AND I CAN DECLARE THEM UNCONSTITUTIONAL

I CAN OVERRIDE THE PRESIDENT'S VETO

I CAN DECLARE EXECUTIVE ACTIONS UNCONSTITUTIONAL

ONLY I CAN DECLARE WAR → BUT I AM THE COMMANDER IN CHIEF

Courts   President   Congress

I CAN DECLARE EXECUTIVE ACTIONS UNCONSTITUTIONAL → BUT I CAN APPOINT JUDGES → AND I MUST APPROVE APPOINTMENTS

I CAN DECLARE LAWS UNCONSTITUTIONAL → BUT I CAN IMPEACH AND REMOVE JUDGES

AND I CAN PROPOSE AMENDMENTS TO THE CONSTITUTION

Each branch has its own special powers. But through a system of checks and balances, these powers are limited by the powers of the other branches. In this way, no branch of government, individual official, or group of people can become too dominant.

The delegates made the new constitution as direct, simple, and flexible as possible. After all, they were designing a government for future generations. Who knew what changes the coming years, decades, and centuries would bring?

Letter (1780)

Telegraph (1844)　　　Telephone (1876)

Computer (1940s)

Cell phone (1973)

They also knew that these future generations would need to occasionally change, or amend, the Constitution. For instance, amendments would gradually extend the right to vote to all adult American citizens.

1800 White men who own land or businesses

1870 Black men (Amendment 15)

1920 Women (Amendment 19)

1971 18-year-olds (Amendment 26)

The Constitution includes the so-called Elastic Clause, which gives Congress the power to make laws that are "necessary and proper" in whatever unforeseen circumstances that may yet arise.

YOU HAVE THE RIGHT TO TRIAL BY JURY.

The last issue to be raised was a bill of rights. Should the Constitution detail a list of guaranteed individual rights?

The delegates voted no. State constitutions already included such a bill of rights, they said. This decision would come back to haunt them.

THIS NEWFANGLED CONSTITUTION DOESN'T SAY I HAVE THE RIGHT TO TRIAL BY JURY?

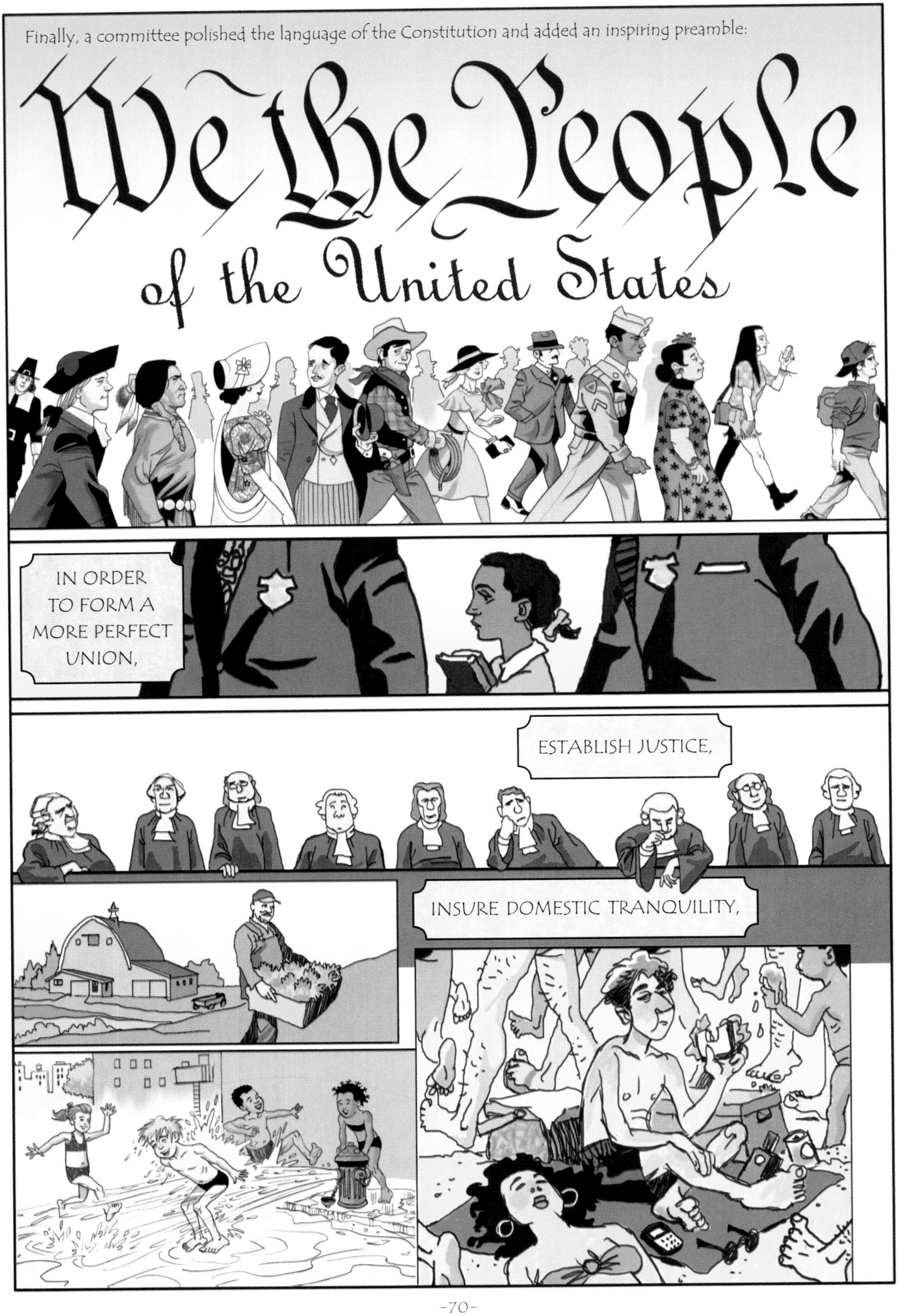
Finally, a committee polished the language of the Constitution and added an inspiring preamble:
We the People
of the United States
IN ORDER TO FORM A MORE PERFECT UNION,
ESTABLISH JUSTICE,
INSURE DOMESTIC TRANQUILITY,

PROVIDE FOR THE COMMON DEFENCE,

PROMOTE THE GENERAL WELFARE,

AND SECURE THE BLESSINGS OF LIBERTY TO OURSELVES AND OUR POSTERITY,

THE CONSTITUTION OF THE UNITED STATES

DO ORDAIN AND ESTABLISH THIS CONSTITUTION FOR THE UNITED STATES OF AMERICA.

State House, Pennsylvania, September 17, 1787. The Constitution was ready for signing. Not all of the original 55 delegates would sign it. Some had already gone home. Others objected to parts of the final document. Benjamin Franklin urged all those present to sign in a show of unanimity.

I CONSENT TO THIS CONSTITUTION BECAUSE I EXPECT NO BETTER, AND BECAUSE I AM NOT SURE THAT IT IS NOT THE BEST.

In the end, 39 framers signed.

I HAVE OFTEN LOOKED AT THAT SUN . . . WITHOUT BEING ABLE TO TELL WHETHER IT WAS RISING OR SETTING . . .

BUT NOW I HAVE THE HAPPINESS TO KNOW IT IS A RISING SUN AND NOT A SETTING SUN.

No longer a secret document, the U.S. Constitution was ready to be presented to the American people. They would decide whether to accept it as the supreme law of the land.

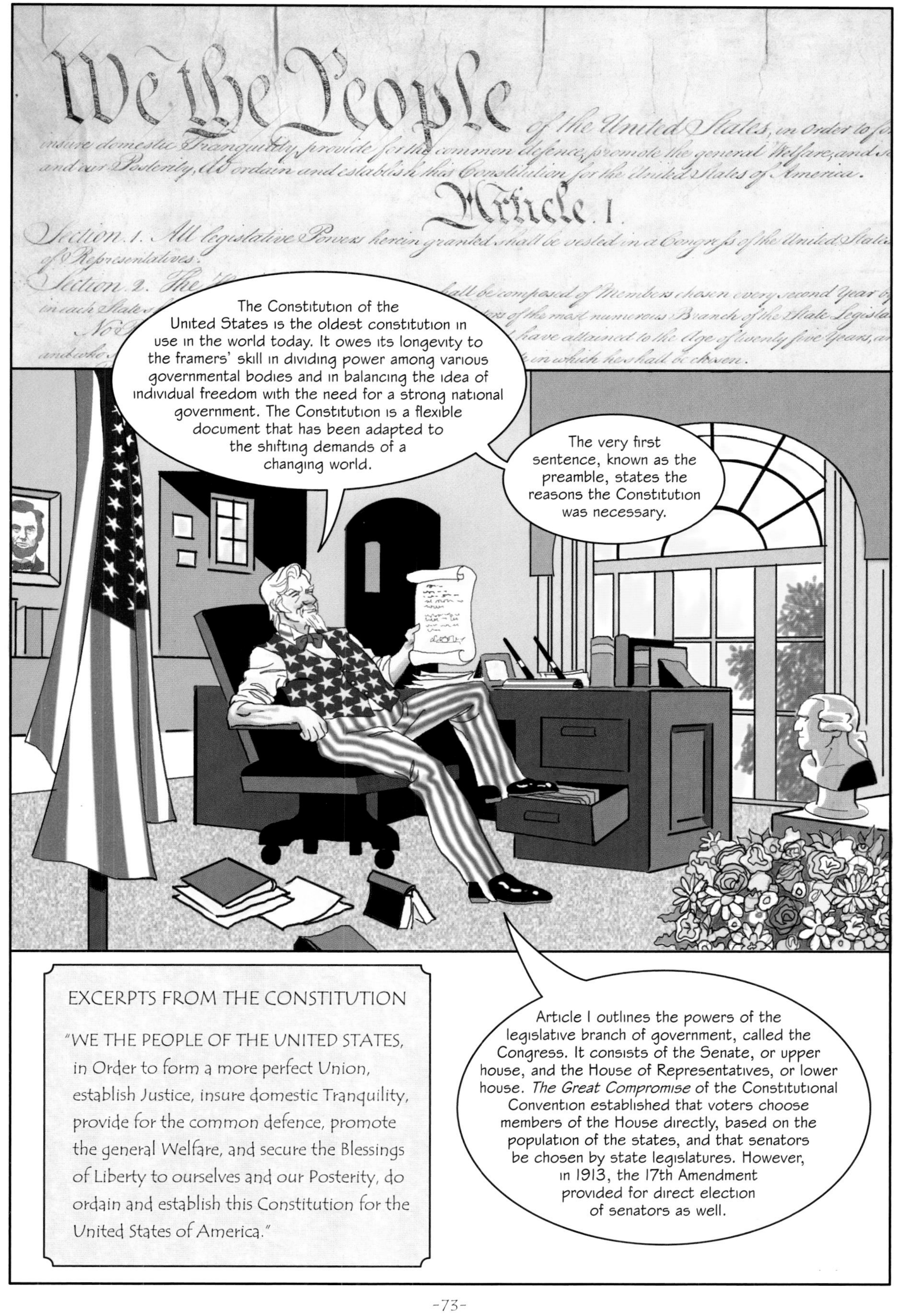
We the People
Article. I
The Constitution of the United States is the oldest constitution in use in the world today. It owes its longevity to the framers' skill in dividing power among various governmental bodies and in balancing the idea of individual freedom with the need for a strong national government. The Constitution is a flexible document that has been adapted to the shifting demands of a changing world.
The very first sentence, known as the preamble, states the reasons the Constitution was necessary.
Article I outlines the powers of the legislative branch of government, called the Congress. It consists of the Senate, or upper house, and the House of Representatives, or lower house. *The Great Compromise* of the Constitutional Convention established that voters choose members of the House directly, based on the population of the states, and that senators be chosen by state legislatures. However, in 1913, the 17th Amendment provided for direct election of senators as well.

EXCERPTS FROM THE CONSTITUTION

"WE THE PEOPLE OF THE UNITED STATES, in Order to form a more perfect Union, establish Justice, insure domestic Tranquility, provide for the common defence, promote the general Welfare, and secure the Blessings of Liberty to ourselves and our Posterity, do ordain and establish this Constitution for the United States of America."

Article II outlines the powers of the executive, or president, and Article III summarizes the powers of the judiciary. Taken together, the first three articles of the Constitution set up a separation of power among the three branches of government. Each branch checks and balances the authority of the other two, so that none is dominant.

The Constitution also divides power between the states and the national government. Some powers are specifically granted to the national government. Those not so assigned are reserved to the states. And some powers are shared by both. This system of shared powers is called *federalism*.

"Article I, Section 8, Clause 18: The Congress shall have the Power . . . To make all Laws which shall be necessary and proper for carrying into Execution the foregoing Powers, and all other Powers vested by this Constitution in the Government of the United States, or in any Department or Officer thereof."

This so-called Elastic Clause gives Congress the freedom to exercise powers and make the kinds of laws not necessarily specified in the Constitution. Over the years, as lawmakers have argued over the extent of federal power, this clause has proved controversial.

Article V details the procedure whereby the Constitution can be amended, or changed. The amendment process is so demanding that only 27 amendments have been passed since 1787.

For the framers of the Constitution, the issue of slavery was extremely controversial. Many states, especially in the South, felt that their economic prosperity depended on the institution of slavery. Most delegates, especially in the North, however, hated to see slavery given official status by the new national government. As a result, slavery is never mentioned by name in the Constitution, and slaves are referred to indirectly as "Persons."

"Representatives and direct Taxes shall be apportioned among the several States which may be included within this Union, according to their respective Numbers, which shall be determined by adding to the whole Number of free Persons, including those bound to Service for a Term of Years, and excluding Indians not taxed, three fifths of all other Persons."

In order to determine the population of each state, each slave would be counted as three-fifths of a person. This was the Three-Fifths Compromise.

"The Migration or Importation of such Persons as any of the States now existing shall think proper to admit, shall not be prohibited by the Congress prior to the Year one thousand eight hundred and eight."

The slave trade could continue, but only until 1808. That year, the import and export of slaves was banned. The institution of slavery, though, continued to divide the nation until the Civil War, in the middle of the 19th century. Slavery was finally abolished by constitutional amendment in 1865.

The slavery passages have since been nullified by the 13th Amendment, which abolished slavery, the 14th Amendment, which granted the rights of citizenship to all persons born in the United States, and the 15th Amendment, which forbade denying the vote to anyone on the basis of "race, color, or previous condition of servitude."

A vigorous public debate followed the signing of the U.S. Constitution, as Americans considered the details of the document and the future of the nation. Since the Constitution needed to be ratified by at least nine states in order to become official, the battle for ratification was fought out state by state. Into the fray jumped James Madison and Alexander Hamilton, who wrote a brilliant series of articles called the Federalist Papers that explained and defended the ideas of the Constitution.

September 19, 1787. Just days after the Constitutional Convention disbanded, the full text of the Constitution began to appear in newspapers throughout the states.

People were shocked and excited by what they read. Few had expected such a radical overhaul of the Confederation government.

We the people

We the People

Immediately, the nation split into two camps. The supporters of the Constitution were called Federalists, and the opponents of the Constitution were called Anti-Federalists. They would confront each other at the ratifying conventions in each state.

RATIFY NOW

PROTECT OUR LIBERTY

DEFEAT THE CONSTITUTION

George Washington

Benjamin Franklin

James Madison

Alexander Hamilton

WE THE PEOPLE!

But the Anti-Federalists claimed the best orator, the fiery Patrick Henry.

Patrick Henry

Samuel Adams

George Mason

WE THE PEOPLE? Whatever happened to WE THE STATES?

Federalists and Anti-Federalists alike gathered their forces for a battle of words. The Federalists were led by the Constitution's framers, the most famous men in America.

The Anti-Federalists had legitimate concerns, all centered on the idea of a too-powerful federal government, which, they believed, would undermine the authority of the states . . .

. . . raise taxes . . .

. . . and concentrate influence in the hands of wealthy politicians and businessmen, far removed from ordinary citizens.

Anti-Federalists were most concerned that the Constitution threatened individual liberties. They felt it needed a bill of rights to defend citizens against the national government.

To win public support for the Constitution, James Madison, Alexander Hamilton, and John Jay wrote 85 essays between October 1787 and March 1788 under the pen name *Publius*. Originally published in newspapers, the Federalist Papers remain an invaluable guide to the intentions of the framers of the Constitution.

November 23, 1787. In Federalist No. 10, Madison made the argument that liberty actually thrives better in a larger republic than in a smaller republic.

People were bound to disagree on many issues, he said. Differences in religion, politics, and especially wealth resulted in *factions*, or special interest groups.

In a republic, citizens elect representatives to stand for them in government. In small republics, such as states, these representatives are more likely to be influenced by a special interest group and to be corrupted.

SAILORS GUILD

MERCHANTS ALLIANCE

But larger republics, such as the U.S. government, have many more competing interests. In such republics, one party cannot "outnumber and oppress" the rest. Minority rights and the spirit of liberty are thereby kept alive in larger republics.

The Federalist Papers helped change many minds in favor of ratification. By June 1788, nine states had ratified. But a truly *United* States required the approval of all. The last two important holdouts were Virginia and New York. In Virginia, Patrick Henry made an impassioned, last-ditch Anti-Federalist appeal.

WHITHER IS THE SPIRIT OF AMERICA GONE? . . . WE DREW THE SPIRIT OF LIBERTY FROM OUR BRITISH ANCESTORS.

BUT NOW, SIR, THE AMERICAN SPIRIT, ASSISTED BY THE ROPES AND CHAINS OF CONSOLIDATION, IS ABOUT TO CONVERT THIS COUNTRY INTO A POWERFUL AND MIGHTY EMPIRE . . .

THERE WILL BE NO CHECKS, NO BALANCES, IN THIS GOVERNMENT.

In his low voice, Madison rebutted Henry's argument, charge by charge.

THE LEGISLATURE WILL BE SUFFICIENT TO CHECK THE POWER OF THE PRESIDENT; THE PRESIDENT, OF THE LEGISLATURE . . .

The Anti-Federalists finally capitulated. But they did so on one condition: a bill of rights had to be added to the Constitution.

I SHALL WAIT IN EXPECTATION OF SEEING THAT GOVERNMENT CHANGED, SO AS TO BE COMPATIBLE WITH THE SAFETY, LIBERTY, AND HAPPINESS OF *THE PEOPLE*.

Bill of Rights

New York City, summer 1788.

With news of Virginia's vote in favor of ratification, New York followed suit. North Carolina and Rhode Island eventually joined them. In festivals and parades across the nation, people cheered the new federal government.

HAMILTON HAMILTON

Federal Hall, New York City, April 30, 1789. As expected, George Washington was unanimously elected to be the first president of the United States. The inauguration took place in New York, the nation's first capital.

I DO SOLEMNLY SWEAR THAT I WILL FAITHFULLY EXECUTE THE OFFICE OF PRESIDENT OF THE UNITED STATES, AND WILL, TO THE BEST OF MY ABILITY, PRESERVE, PROTECT, AND DEFEND THE CONSTITUTION OF THE UNITED STATES. SO HELP ME GOD.

A new nation had been born.

In Federalist No. 10, Madison asserted that the numerous competing factions in a large republic will check one another, resulting in increased liberty and stability. Majorities in larger republics will therefore be less able to impose their will on minorities than in a small republic.

He assumed that conflicts between factions would result in compromises.

EXCERPT FROM FEDERALIST No. 10

"Hence, it clearly appears, that the same advantage which a republic has over a democracy, in controlling the effects of faction, is enjoyed by a large over a small republic--is enjoyed by the Union over the States composing it . . . The influence of factious leaders may kindle a flame within their particular States, but will be unable to spread a general conflagration through the other States . . . In the extent and proper structure of the Union, therefore, we behold a republican remedy for the diseases most incident to republican government. And according to the degree of pleasure and pride we feel in being republicans, ought to be our zeal in cherishing the spirit and supporting the character of Federalists."

The individual liberties that Americans cherish as their birthright were discussed but ultimately not included in the original Constitution. Rather, they are enshrined in the first ten amendments, known collectively as the Bill of Rights. Many states ratified the Constitution only after they were assured that a bill of rights would be added immediately. And so it was.

New York City, March 1789. As soon as New York ratified the Constitution, congressional elections were held throughout the thirteen states. By the following spring, new congressmen were arriving in New York City, the new nation's first capital. Their first order of business was passing a bill of rights.

Among the new representatives was James Madison of Virginia. Partly at the urging of his friend Thomas Jefferson, he decided to sponsor the amendments.

A BILL OF RIGHTS IS WHAT THE PEOPLE ARE ENTITLED TO AGAINST EVERY GOVERNMENT ON EARTH . . . AND WHAT NO JUST GOVERNMENT SHOULD REFUSE.

Madison knew that these amendments were necessary to increase support for the Constitution among Anti-Federalists and the general public.

On June 8, 1789, Madison introduced his amendments as the Bill of Rights and passionately argued in their defense.

YOU SHOULD DECLARE THE GREAT RIGHTS OF MANKIND SECURED UNDER THE CONSTITUTION.

Madison found inspiration in different sources. The oldest was England's Magna Carta of 1215. It stated that no man could be "captured or imprisoned" except by "lawful judgment of his peers" or the "law of the land."

THE KING MUST GRANT CERTAIN BASIC RIGHTS TO HIS PEOPLE. SIGN HERE.

I'LL SIGN IF I HAVE TO.

For months, the House and the Senate debated, rewrote, and finally accepted a bill of rights. In substance, it was similar to Madison's original version.

In October 1789, President Washington sent the amendments to the states for ratification. When three-quarters of the states accepted them, they became the law of the land.

THERE IS *NO FREEDOM OF THE PRESS* FOR ABOLITIONISTS IN MISSOURI!

On December 15, 1791, the Bill of Rights took effect. At first, only the federal government was required to observe its rules on individual freedoms and rights. State governments were not. For instance, in the 1830s anti-abolitionists burned down Elijah Lovejoy's anti-slavery newspaper.

This was true. But the passage of the 14th Amendment in 1868, and numerous judicial decisions since, gradually established that states must also abide by the Bill of Rights.

And now, here is *your* Bill of Rights.

FIRST AMENDMENT

The First Amendment guarantees freedom of religion, speech, and the press, the right to assemble, and the right to petition.

Freedom of Religion. Congress cannot interfere with freedom of worship. Before the Bill of Rights, the idea of religious freedom had gained ground because people of so many different faiths had come to America.

Today, Americans of diverse religions worship as they choose.

Congress also cannot establish an official state religion the way Britain's King Henry VIII did when he founded the Church of England. Nor can it compel people to observe certain religious customs.

Church of England

Church of America

Thomas Jefferson said that the Establishment Clause erected a "wall of separation between church and state."

NOT ALLOWING ME TO PRAY WOULD VIOLATE *MY* CONSTITUTIONAL RIGHTS!

FORCING ME TO PRAY VIOLATES MY CONSTITUTIONAL RIGHTS!

But how high is that wall? For the past 50 years, there has been much controversy involving religion in government-sponsored institutions, such as public schools.

Freedom of Speech. The First Amendment also protects the right of free speech. Citizens have the right to express their opinions even when others disagree or find their opinions offensive.

BUT THE FIRST AMENDMENT WILL NOT PROTECT SOMEONE FALSELY SHOUTING "FIRE" IN A CROWDED THEATER.

FIRE!

The amendment has been interpreted to have limits, such as in the case of speech that causes a "clear and present danger," which *can* be prohibited.

SNCC

Certain kinds of nonverbal speech are also protected. For instance, during the Vietnam War, the Supreme Court ruled that students had the right to wear black armbands to protest the war.

Freedom of the press. In the early colonies, newspapers could print only material that had been approved by the British government. Precedents for freedom of the press began with the trial of the New York printer John Peter Zenger in 1734.

James Madison and the founders believed that a free press was necessary to the security of a nation. It fosters public discussion about current events and pressures the government into doing its job right.

BECAUSE ZENGER'S CRITICISM OF OUR BRITISH GOVERNOR IS TRUE, HE CANNOT BE PROSECUTED FOR LIBEL!

NEW YORK POST

Vote for Romney!

The New York Times

Vote for Obama!

Today these press freedoms apply not only to newspapers and books but also to TV, radio, movies, and the Internet.

THE FEDERAL EMERGENCY RESPONSE TO HURRICANE KATRINA HAS BEEN SLOW AND TOTALLY INADEQUATE.

CNN

Right of Peaceful Assembly. People have the right to hold public meetings and demonstrations, whether to protest unfair working conditions, march for civil rights, or nominate political leaders.

SOMEWHERE I READ OF THE FREEDOM OF ASSEMBLY. SOMEWHERE I READ OF THE FREEDOM OF SPEECH . . . SOMEWHERE I READ THAT THE GREATNESS OF AMERICA IS THE RIGHT TO PROTEST FOR RIGHT.

CONGRESSMAN SMITH

Right of Petition. People also have the right to contact government officials to petition for change.

WOULD YOU SIGN THIS PETITION TO BAN NUCLEAR POWER STATIONS IN YOUR STATE?

First Amendment rights are not absolute, however. Individual rights end where the rights of others begin. Sometimes it is hard to determine where that line is.

THE CONSTITUTION GIVES ME THE *RIGHT* TO PROTEST ON THIS STREET!

YOUR PROTEST VIOLATES MY RIGHT TO GO TO WORK.

OCCUPY WALL STREET

WE ARE THE 99%

JORDAN MARKET

POLICE

SECOND AMENDMENT

The Second Amendment deals with the right to keep and bear arms. Rather than have the federal government maintain a large standing army, the founders felt it was important for states to raise their own militias, or groups of civilian soldiers.

However, because the phrasing of the amendment is ambiguous, judicial scholars and politicians have long argued about its meaning.

Did the founders mean to emphasize the collective right of state militias . . .

The Second Amendment ties the right to carry guns to the need to maintain a militia.

. . . or the right of each individual citizen to own a gun?

When gun violence does occur, state and national legislatures debate anew about possible limits on the right to bear arms.

The Third Amendment says that soldiers will not be housed in private homes unless the owner agrees. This addressed the forced lodging of British soldiers in the homes of the colonists under the Coercive Acts but has not been relevant since.

The Fourth Amendment protects people's property, papers, and bodies from "unreasonable searches and seizures."

For instance, it prevents law enforcement officials from entering private homes unless they have a search warrant . . .

Sometimes the government must balance the need for national security against Fourth Amendment rights. In the 21st century, Congress has passed antiterrorism laws that allow the government to eavesdrop on private phone and Internet communication.

The Fifth Amendment guarantees the right to fair treatment under the law.

No one can be deprived of "life, liberty, or property" without due process, or a series of approved legal procedures.

When is collective security more important than an individual's right to privacy? The debate continues.

YOUR PRELIMINARY HEARING WILL BE HELD TOMORROW. THE JUDGE WILL DECIDE WHETHER THERE IS SUFFICIENT EVIDENCE THAT YOU HAVE COMMITTED A CRIME.

Nor can anyone be tried twice in criminal court for the same crime, known as *double jeopardy*.

WE FIND THE DEFENDANT NOT GUILTY.

No one can be forced to testify against themselves; they have the right to remain silent.

I REFUSE TO ANSWER ON THE GROUNDS THAT I MAY INCRIMINATE MYSELF.

Refusing to answer a question during a legal proceeding is called taking the Fifth.

The Fifth Amendment also says that government cannot take away people's property without paying them for it.

BUT THIS HIGHWAY IS GOING RIGHT THROUGH MY LAND!

DON'T WORRY, THE GOVERNMENT WILL COMPENSATE YOU.

SIXTH AMENDMENT

The Sixth Amendment specifies the rights of someone accused of a crime.

The accused must have a "speedy and public trial" by an impartial jury--a jury that does not have any preconceived ideas about guilt or innocence.

YES, I HAVE A VERY STRONG OPINION ABOUT JAYWALKERS. I THINK THEY SHOULD ALL GO TO PRISON!

YOU ARE DISMISSED FROM JURY DUTY.

The accused has the right to be told why he was arrested . . .

YOU HAVE BEEN ACCUSED OF BREAKING AND ENTERING.

. . . and the right to a lawyer. In 1963, this right was extended even to those who cannot afford a lawyer.

YOU HAVE THE RIGHT TO AN ATTORNEY. IF YOU CANNOT AFFORD AN ATTORNEY, ONE WILL BE APPOINTED FOR YOU.

SEVENTH AMENDMENT

The Seventh Amendment also provides for jury trials in federal noncriminal, or civil, trials.

EIGHTH AMENDMENT

The Eighth Amendment prohibits excessive bail and fines.

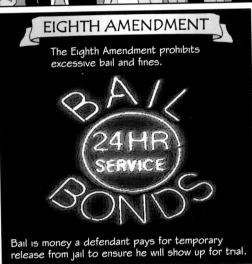

Bail is money a defendant pays for temporary release from jail to ensure he will show up for trial.

The Eighth Amendment also forbids "cruel and unusual punishments." A cruel punishment is one that causes an excessive amount of pain.

Although the death penalty is legal in most states, there is still a vigorous debate over whether it constitutes "cruel and unusual" punishment.

NINTH AMENDMENT

The Ninth Amendment states that the people also have rights that are not specifically mentioned in the Constitution. The framers knew that even a bill of rights could not possibly name all the personal freedoms people should possess.

For instance, in 1965 in *Griswold v. Connecticut*, the Supreme Court decided that married people possess a right to privacy. Although this right is not explicitly mentioned in the Bill of Rights, it is implied.

TENTH AMENDMENT

The Tenth Amendment states that any powers not granted to the federal government or denied to the states belong to the states or to the people.

It reaffirms the principle of federalism that Madison and others advanced in the *Federalist Papers*: the division of power between the national and the state governments. It also discourages the federal government from interfering on issues that states will never agree on.

THE COURT STRIKES DOWN THE FEDERAL LAW CREATING GUN-FREE SCHOOL ZONES. SUCH LAWS ARE UP TO STATE AND LOCAL GOVERNMENTS.

The first ten amendments define Americans' conception of freedom. Over the years, the Supreme Court has interpreted each of these amendments in a series of landmark court cases, extending the protections of the Bill of Rights to all Americans, including women, African Americans, and other minorities. Groups of citizens have sometimes disagreed with the decisions the court has handed down, and the issues they raise have been hotly contested in public debate.

Amendment 1

"Congress shall make no law respecting an establishment of religion, or prohibiting the free exercise thereof; or abridging the freedom of speech, or of the press; or the right of the people peaceably to assemble, and to petition the Government for a redress of grievances."

Amendment 2

"A well regulated Militia, being necessary to the security of a free State, the right of the people to keep and bear Arms, shall not be infringed."

Amendment 3

"No Soldier shall, in time of peace be quartered in any house, without the consent of the Owner, nor in time of war, but in a manner to be prescribed by law."

Amendment 4

"The right of the people to be secure in their persons, houses, papers, and effects, against unreasonable searches and seizures, shall not be violated, and no Warrants shall issue, but upon probable cause, supported by Oath or affirmation, and particularly describing the place to be searched, and the persons or things to be seized."

Amendment 5

"No person shall be held to answer for a capital, or otherwise infamous crime, unless on a presentment or indictment of a Grand Jury, except in cases arising in the land or naval forces, or in the Militia, when in actual service in time of War or public danger; nor shall any person be subject for the same offence to be twice put in jeopardy of life or limb; nor shall be compelled in any criminal case to be a witness against himself, nor be deprived of life, liberty, or property, without due process of law; nor shall private property be taken for public use, without just compensation."

Amendment 6

"In all criminal prosecutions, the accused shall enjoy the right to a speedy and public trial, by an impartial jury of the State and district wherein the crime shall have been committed . . . and to be informed of the nature and cause of the accusation; to be confronted with the witnesses against him; to have compulsory process for obtaining witnesses in his favor, and to have the Assistance of Counsel for his defence."

Amendment 7

"In suits at common law, where the value in controversy shall exceed twenty dollars, the right of trial by jury shall be preserved, and no fact tried by a jury, shall be otherwise reexamined in any Court of the United States, than according to the rules of the common law."

Amendment 8

"Excessive bail shall not be required, nor excessive fines imposed, nor cruel and unusual punishments inflicted."

Amendment 9

"The enumeration in the Constitution, of certain rights, shall not be construed to deny or disparage others retained by the people."

Amendment 10

"The powers not delegated to the United States by the Constitution, nor prohibited by it to the States, are reserved to the States respectively, or to the people."

When Washington took office, he knew that all his actions would set a precedent for future generations.

I WALK ON UNTRODDEN GROUND.

George Washington took office as president of the United States in 1789 in an atmosphere of goodwill and universal approval. Yet by the end of eight years, the nation was split into two bitterly divided political parties and threatened by a combustible European war. In his Farewell Address of 1796, Washington used the experience he had gained during his difficult tenure to offer his best advice to the young nation.

But as the country's first president, he knew he was going to need help. He already had John Adams by his side as vice president. He then appointed the most able men he knew to his cabinet, including Thomas Jefferson as secretary of state and Alexander Hamilton as secretary of the Treasury.

Thomas Jefferson, a member of the Virginia planter elite, authored the Declaration of Independence and was the former U.S. ambassador to France. To his new position he brought strong convictions about individuals' and states' rights.

Alexander Hamilton, born in the West Indies and educated in New York, was Washington's closest aide during the Revolution. He planned to develop an economic policy that would make the United States a prosperous nation.

Paris, July 14, 1789. Just three months after Washington's inauguration, France exploded into revolution. The lower and middle classes rose up against the privileged and wealthy.

France had aided America in its fight for independence. Would Americans support the French Revolution's fight for liberty and equality in return?

The answer would not become apparent immediately, because America faced a more pressing problem at home. Alexander Hamilton estimated that the nation and individual states together owed a total of $77 million in wartime debt, both to foreign countries and to individual investors.

DEBT

Hamilton wanted the federal government to assume all debt, both state and federal. Some congressmen, such as Virginia's James Madison, objected. This plan would give the national government too much economic power over the states.

LET THE NORTHERN STATES TAKE RESPONSIBILITY FOR THEIR OWN DEBTS.

Also, various Southern states had already repaid most of what they owed.

New York City, June 20, 1790.

At dinner one night, Jefferson suggested a compromise.

IF MR. MADISON DROPS HIS OPPOSITION TO THE BILL, PERHAPS MR. HAMILTON COULD SUPPORT OUR SCHEME TO LOCATE THE NEW CAPITAL IN THE SOUTH.

Accordingly, Hamilton's debt bill passed, and a new national capital would be built on the Potomac River between Virginia and Maryland.

Hamilton's next proposal--a national bank of the United States--was even more controversial.

THE CONSTITUTION SAYS NOTHING ABOUT A NATIONAL BANK. CREATING ONE WOULD BE UNCONSTITUTIONAL!

REMEMBER THAT THE CONSTITUTION GIVES THE GOVERNMENT THE POWER TO TAKE ALL "NECESSARY AND PROPER" STEPS TO CARRY OUT ITS DUTIES.

Hamilton pushed the bank bill through.

Paris, January 1793.

Meanwhile, the French Revolution was hijacked by radicals, who began a "Reign of Terror." All suspected opponents of the Revolution, including King Louis XVI, faced *la guillotine.*

Fearing the spread of revolution across Europe, Great Britain and other monarchies launched a concerted attack on France.

British

Austrian

Russian

Many Americans felt they should come to France's aid.

Thomas Jefferson was ardently pro-France. Despite the violence of the Revolution, he believed that it promoted human liberty and democracy.

Hamilton was pro-British. Britain, after all, was America's most important trading partner. Also, like Washington, he feared the lawlessness of mob rule.

Washington recognized that his nation was too weak to go to war against England. In April 1793, he issued the Neutrality Proclamation, stating that the United States would not take sides in the war.

NEUTRALITY PROCLAMATION

IT IS THE SINCERE WISH OF UNITED AMERICA TO HAVE NOTHING TO DO WITH...THE SQUABBLES OF EUROPEAN NATIONS.

The proclamation caused a storm of protest.

FRANCE AND AMERICA, ALLIES FOREVER!

FILTHY JACOBIN!

MIND YOUR TONGUE, YOU BRITISH BOOT-LICKER!

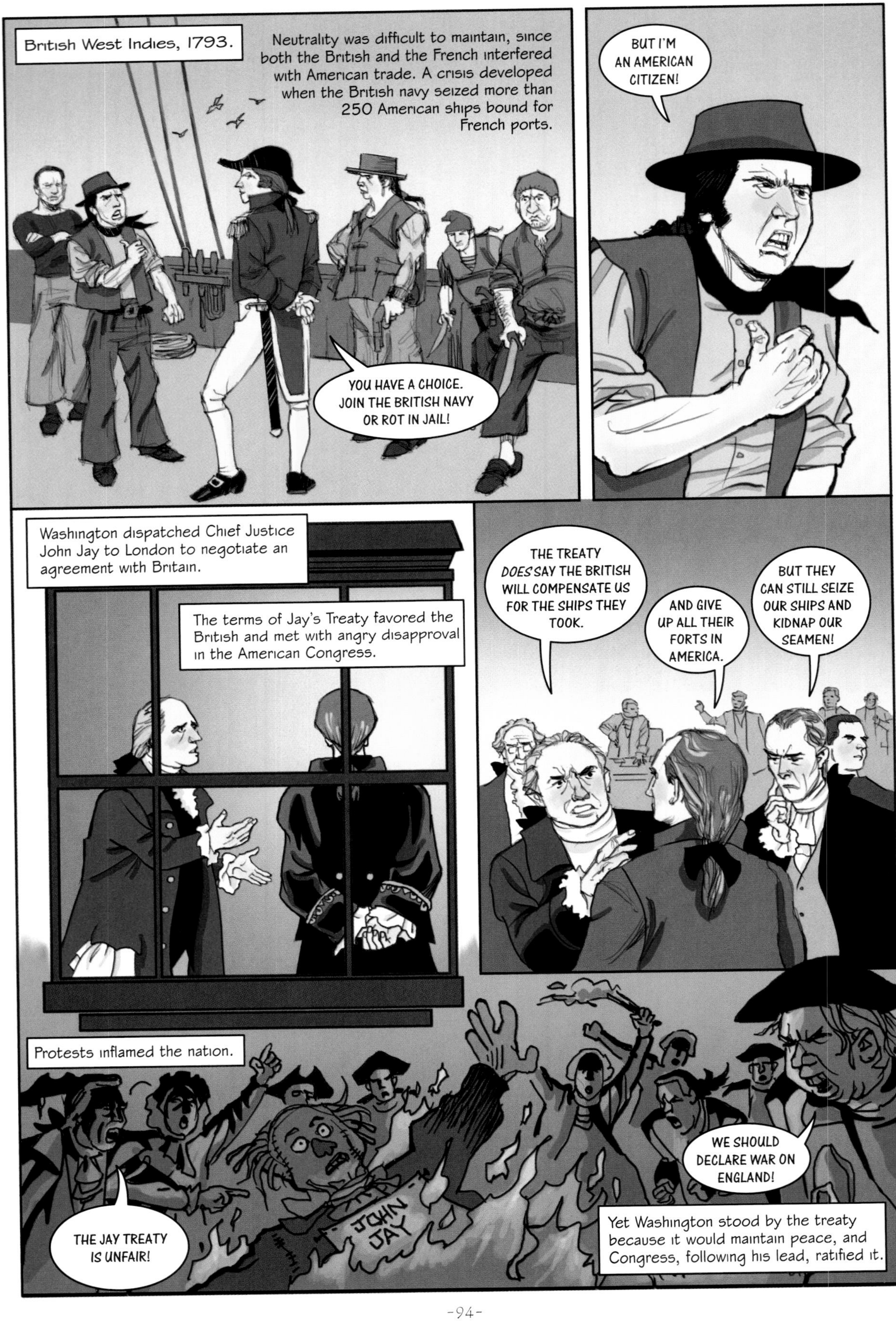
British West Indies, 1793.
Neutrality was difficult to maintain, since both the British and the French interfered with American trade. A crisis developed when the British navy seized more than 250 American ships bound for French ports.
YOU HAVE A CHOICE. JOIN THE BRITISH NAVY OR ROT IN JAIL!
BUT I'M AN AMERICAN CITIZEN!
Washington dispatched Chief Justice John Jay to London to negotiate an agreement with Britain.
The terms of Jay's Treaty favored the British and met with angry disapproval in the American Congress.
THE TREATY *DOES* SAY THE BRITISH WILL COMPENSATE US FOR THE SHIPS THEY TOOK.
AND GIVE UP ALL THEIR FORTS IN AMERICA.
BUT THEY CAN STILL SEIZE OUR SHIPS AND KIDNAP OUR SEAMEN!
Protests inflamed the nation.
JOHN JAY
THE JAY TREATY IS UNFAIR!
WE SHOULD DECLARE WAR ON ENGLAND!
Yet Washington stood by the treaty because it would maintain peace, and Congress, following his lead, ratified it.

By Washington's second term, major disagreements within the government had led to the formation of America's first political parties. Alexander Hamilton led the Federalist Party, which called for a strong central, or federal, government.

Federalist Party

Democratic Republican Party

Thomas Jefferson and James Madison led the Democratic-Republican Party, which supported strong state governments.

Hamilton foresaw an urban, cosmopolitan nation powered by strong manufacturing and trade and led by the political, business, and intellectual elite.

Jefferson envisioned a democratic, egalitarian society supported by independent farmers and a knowledgeable, middle-class citizenry.

Each party attracted avid supporters and a fiercely partisan press.

NATIONAL GAZETTE

GAZETTE OF THE UNITED STATES

After Jay's Treaty, Democratic-Republican newspapers published a stream of abuse directed at the president.

NATIONAL GAZETTE

These personal attacks helped Washington make up his mind. After two terms, he longed for a return to private life.

His Farewell Address urged all citizens to act as one unified nation and not allow themselves to be divided by unimportant differences.

UNITY OF GOVERNMENT IS THE MAIN PROP OF YOUR LIBERTY.

On September 19, 1796, Washington published an open letter to the American people.

Washington warned Americans to beware the "spirit of party." Partisan politics turned people of one region, religion, or interest group against another.

TRAITOR!
UN-AMERICAN!
CORRUPT!
TRAITOR!
UNGODLY!
UN-AMERICAN!
CORRUPT!
UNGODLY!

POLITICAL DIVIDING LINE

Washington cautioned that such hostility can lead to conflict or even open rebellion.

Washington ended by saying that the United States should avoid lasting foreign alliances. The interests of European nations could not be those of America.

Then, after 20 years in the service of his country, Washington retired.

The ideas expressed in the Farewell Address have directed the nation ever since, though they are continually debated and reconsidered.

Alexander Hamilton wrote most of the actual words of the address, although he was expressing Washington's ideas. They collaborated on the final text.

Washington believed that political parties, with their conflicting views, weakened the unity of the nation. By contrast, in Federalist No. 10, James Madison argued that it was necessary to have many different political ideas expressed by a wide range of people in order to prevent the tyranny of the majority.

EXCERPTS FROM WASHINGTON'S FAREWELL ADDRESS

"The spirit of party... serves always to distract the public councils and enfeeble the public administration. It agitates the community with ill-founded jealousies and false alarms, kindles the animosity of one part against another, foments occasionally riot and insurrection. It opens the door to foreign influence and corruption."

Washington reacted to the American foreign policy dilemma posed by the French Revolution by advocating that Americans never choose permanent foreign partners. His words about avoiding American alliances have encouraged American isolationists to the present day. Thomas Jefferson would later call partnerships that might harm American interests "entangling alliances."

"...The great rule of conduct for us in regard to foreign nations is in extending our commercial relations to have with them as little political connection as possible... It is our true policy to steer clear of permanent alliances with any portion of the foreign world... Nothing is more essential than that permanent, inveterate antipathies against particular nations, and passionate attachments for others, should be excluded; and that, in place of them, just and amicable feelings towards all should be cultivated."

Jefferson's First Inaugural Address

1801 was an amazing year.

After a vicious election campaign, Thomas Jefferson became the third president of the United States--and control of the government passed peaceably from one political party to another. In his inaugural address, Jefferson tried to unite a divided country and signaled the major themes of his administration.

At the turn of the new century, Federalists and Democratic-Republicans--also known as Republicans*-- disagreed on practically everything.

FEDERALISTS	DEMOCRATIC- REPUBLICANS
STRONG CENTRAL GOVERNMENT	STRONG STATE GOVERNMENTS
$ FAVORED BUSINESS INTERESTS	FAVORED FARMING INTERESTS
PRO-BRITISH	PRO-FRENCH
LOOSE CONSTRUCTION OF THE CONSTITUTION	STRICT CONSTRUCTION OF THE CONSTITUTION 

Their bitter rivalry had begun during Washington's presidency and continued under the second president, John Adams, who was a Federalist.

A Republican and a Federalist even came to blows in the House of Representatives.

I SPIT UPON YOU, SIR!

YOU ARE A REPUBLICAN SCOUNDREL, SIR!

SURRENDER AND PREPARE TO BE BOARDED!

President Adams's biggest challenges arose from the ongoing war between France and Britain. After the United States signed the Jay Treaty with Britain in 1794, France began to seize American ships on the high seas.

*Not to be confused with today's Republican Party.

Summer 1798.

MILLIONS FOR DEFENSE...

NOT ONE CENT FOR TRIBUTE!

Wanting to preserve peace, Adams sent diplomats to negotiate with France's minister of foreign affairs, Talleyrand. When the minister's three agents (referred to as X, Y, and Z) demanded a bribe in return for a treaty, the American public was outraged.

Indignant citizens, especially Federalists, said they would rather go to war than allow France to extort and humiliate the United States.

After the so-called XYZ Affair, an undeclared war with France -- the "Quasi-War"-- raged for two years. American ships hunted down French privateers and captured them.

Federalists in Congress raised taxes to build up an American navy. Adams did not want a real war, however, and would eventually sign a treaty with France.

1798. Congress, controlled by Federalists, struck back at political attacks in the Republican press by passing repressive laws called the Alien and Sedition Acts.

GAZETTE OF THE UNITED STATES

NATIONAL GAZETTE

The Alien Act made it harder to become an American citizen and gave the president the right to deport "dangerous" foreigners. President Adams never expelled anyone, though. The Sedition Act made it illegal to criticize the government.

Leading Republicans retaliated. They argued that individual states had the right to nullify federal laws they disagreed with.

THE SEDITION ACT ATTACKS FREE SPEECH AND FREEDOM OF THE PRESS!

Under the Sedition Act, 25 people were tried, and 10 went to jail, most of them Republican newspaper editors.

Virginia and Kentucky passed resolutions, written by Madison and Jefferson, declaring that states could decide that a law was unconstitutional.

The 1800 elections took place in an exceptionally contentious atmosphere. The Federalist candidate for president was once again John Adams, with Charles Pinckney running for vice president. The Republican candidates were Thomas Jefferson for president and Aaron Burr for vice president.

Although the race was close, the Republicans beat the Federalists. But Jefferson and Burr each had 73 votes in the Electoral College!*

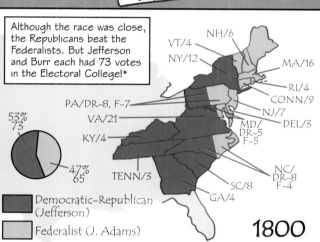

53%
73

47%
65

Democratic-Republican (Jefferson)

Federalist (J. Adams)

1800

According to the Constitution, the House of Representatives had the responsibility to break a tie in the Electoral College.

The House voted 35 times--and remained deadlocked.

The stalemate was broken by advice from the leading Federalist, Alexander Hamilton. He had known both men a long time, and he despised the ambitious, slippery Aaron Burr.

JEFFERSON IS TO BE PREFERRED. HE IS BY FAR NOT SO DANGEROUS A MAN.

The antagonism between Hamilton and Burr continued to grow.

Four years later, Burr challenged Hamilton to a duel and killed him.

"REJOICE! COLUMBIA'S SONS, REJOICE!

TO TYRANTS NEVER BEND THE KNEE,

BUT JOIN WITH HEART AND SOUL AND VOICE

FOR **JEFFERSON** AND **LIBERTY** . . ."

February 17, 1801. Finally, on the 36th ballot, Thomas Jefferson was elected president by one vote. A popular song celebrated his victory.

* The Constitution called for electors to submit two names. The winner would be president and the runner-up would be vice president. To prevent future ties, the 12th Amendment was passed in 1804 allowing electors to vote separately for president and vice president.

March 4, 1801.

Jefferson walked the short distance from his lodgings to the unfinished Capitol building for his inauguration.

He purposely made his "little parade" as plain and unassuming as possible. He wanted Republican simplicity to contrast favorably with the relative formality of Washington's and Adams's inaugurals.

After he took his oath of office, Jefferson delivered his inauguration address in the Senate chamber.

WE HAVE CALLED BY DIFFERENT NAMES BRETHREN OF THE SAME PRINCIPLE. WE ARE ALL REPUBLICANS, WE ARE ALL FEDERALISTS.

He emphasized Republican principles of minimal government, individual freedom, and low taxes.

A WISE AND FRUGAL GOVERNMENT . . . WHICH SHALL LEAVE MEN OTHERWISE FREE TO REGULATE THEIR OWN PURSUITS OF INDUSTRY AND IMPROVEMENT . . . THIS IS THE SUM OF GOOD GOVERNMENT.

The author of the Declaration of Independence, President Jefferson, also stressed freedom of religion, of the press, and "of person."

THE SEDITION ACT IS NO LONGER ENFORCED. YOU ARE FREE TO GO.

A relieved country celebrated the smooth transition to a new presidency. One observer of Jefferson's inauguration, Margaret Bayard Smith, marveled at the unprecedented occasion:

THE CHANGES OF ADMINISTRATION WHICH IN EVERY GOVERNMENT AND IN EVERY AGE HAVE GENERALLY BEEN EPOCHS OF CONFUSION, VILLAINY, AND BLOODSHED, IN THIS OUR HAPPY COUNTRY TAKE PLACE WITHOUT ANY SPECIES OF DISTRACTION, OR DISORDER.

Jefferson called his election the "revolution of 1800" because he believed he was returning the nation to the principles of the American Revolution. The peaceful transition he led to a new government under a different political party set a precedent for every president since. Through his conciliatory words, Jefferson reminded members of both political parties of their common devotion to the principles of republicanism and federalism.

EXCERPTS FROM JEFFERSON'S
FIRST INAUGURAL ADDRESS

"Let us, then, fellow-citizens, unite with one heart and one mind. Let us restore to social intercourse that harmony and affection without which liberty and even life itself are but dreary things . . . But every difference of opinion is not a difference of principle. We have called by different names brethren of the same principle. We are all Republicans, we are all Federalists."

Jefferson articulated the democratic principles of free speech and the right to dissent, as well as his belief in a smaller and simpler federal government and low taxes.

"It is proper you should understand what I deem the essential principles of our Government, and consequently those which ought to shape its Administration . . . Equal and exact justice to all men, of whatever state or persuasion, religious or political; peace, commerce, and honest friendship with all nations, entangling alliances with none."

The Constitution established an independent federal judiciary but left the powers of the Supreme Court--and the lower federal courts--somewhat vague. Through their decisions, the courts ultimately defined and refined their role. Possibly the most important of all Supreme Court cases was *Marbury v. Madison*, which established the power of *judicial review*.

John Adams lost the opportunity to serve a second term as president when Thomas Jefferson won the election in 1800. But just before Adams left office, the position of chief justice of the Supreme Court opened up.

Newspaper Gazette

JEFFERSON WINS PRESIDENCY

January 21, 1801.

Adams nominated his secretary of state, John Marshall--a former leader of the Federalist Party in Virginia--to fill the vacancy.

JOHN MARSHALL IS CONFIRMED AS CHIEF JUSTICE OF THE SUPREME COURT.

Fair-minded and intellectually agile, John Marshall was proud of his service with General Washington in the American Revolution.

He would guide the Supreme Court for 34 years, judging 1,100 cases and writing 519 decisions. Many consider him the greatest chief justice in American history.

Like Adams, Marshall believed that a strong federal judiciary provided an effective balance to the power of the legislature and the presidency.

Because they were appointed for life, justices would be less likely to be swayed by changes in public opinion.

In his final weeks in office, Adams also appointed 42 new district judges. Naturally, they were all Federalists. The Republican press sneered that a desperate Adams had used the last moments of his presidency to appoint these so-called *midnight judges*.

The incoming president, Thomas Jefferson, resented all of Adams's Federalist appointments. He *particularly* disliked Marshall, his distant cousin, because of the way Marshall could "twist" any argument to his advantage.

WHEN CONVERSING WITH MARSHALL, I NEVER ADMIT ANYTHING. IF HE WERE TO ASK ME IF IT WERE DAYLIGHT OR NOT, I'D REPLY, "SIR, I DON'T KNOW."

Jefferson was also suspicious of a strong federal judiciary. He thought it concentrated too much power in the hands of lifetime appointees who were not accountable to the American people.

LOOK AT ALL THE NEW JUDGESHIPS PRESIDENT ADAMS CREATED.

Adams signed and sealed the commissions for the new judges, but since most were not delivered, the new secretary of state, James Madison, found many of the commissions still on the desk when he arrived at his office.

DON'T DELIVER THOSE COMMISSIONS! THEY ARE FEDERAL JUDGESHIPS FOR FEDERALIST JUDGES.

I WON'T.

One of the "midnight judges" who did not get his commission was William Marbury, appointed as justice of the peace for the District of Columbia. He petitioned the Supreme Court to force the Jefferson administration to give him his new job.

The Judiciary Act of 1789 said that as an officeholder, Marbury had the right to appeal to the Supreme Court. After all, despite the commission not being delivered, the president had appointed him.

The case was decided by the Supreme Court in February 1803. Chief Justice Marshall wrote a three-part decision.

First, the court decided that under the Judiciary Act, Marbury did indeed have the right to his new job, since President Adams had signed and sealed the commission.

Then Marshall lectured President Jefferson about his duty to carry out the law:

"THE VERY ESSENCE OF CIVIL LIBERTY CERTAINLY CONSISTS IN THE RIGHT OF EVERY INDIVIDUAL TO CLAIM THE PROTECTION OF THE LAWS."

However, the Supreme Court said the Judiciary Act of 1789 was itself unconstitutional because it violated the separation of powers defined in the Constitution. Marbury had no right to petition the Supreme Court directly.

JUDICIARY ACT OF 1789

This was the first time the Supreme Court had called a congressional law unconstitutional. *Marbury* v. *Madison* set an important precedent for *judicial* review. This is the idea that the Supreme Court has the power to determine whether a congressional act or presidential policy has a basis in the Constitution and to overturn it if it does not. Thus the court acts as a check on both the legislative and executive branches of government.

UNCONSTITUTIONAL!

Since 1803, the Supreme Court has often used judicial review to overturn laws. For instance, in 1997 it overturned the Communications Decency Act of 1996, which attempted to protect children from viewing or reading obscenity on the Internet. The court ruled that the law reduced free speech rights guaranteed by the First Amendment.

Marbury v. Madison established the principle of judicial review as a clearly defined power of the Supreme Court to review the constitutionality of all laws, including federal laws. The Supreme Court is the final authority on all such matters.

EXCERPT FROM *MARBURY V. MADISON*

"It is emphatically the province and duty of the Judicial Department to say what the law is. Those who apply the rule to particular cases must, of necessity, expound and interpret that rule. If two laws conflict with each other, the Courts must decide on the operation of each.

"So, if a law be in opposition to the Constitution . . . the Court must either decide that case conformably to the law, disregarding the Constitution, or conformably to the Constitution, disregarding the law; the Court must determine which of these conflicting rules governs the case. This is of the very essence of judicial duty."

The Louisiana Purchase

In 1803, President Thomas Jefferson made a daring decision that doubled the size of the United States. The Louisiana Purchase was a triumph for the new republic. Young America was restless, always on the move.

In the 1790s, pioneers like Daniel Boone trekked west across the Appalachian Mountains toward the Mississippi River Valley. By 1800, three new states--Kentucky, Tennessee, and Vermont--had entered the Union. More would soon follow.

President Jefferson had ambitious plans for the huge continent, what he called this "empire of liberty."

OUR NATION MUST BE VIEWED AS THE NEST FROM WHICH *ALL* AMERICA, NORTH AND SOUTH, IS TO BE PEOPLED.

Hudson Bay

Pacific Ocean

CANADA

Atlantic Ocean

LOUISIANA

UNITED STATES

NEW SPAIN

FLORIDA

Gulf of Mexico

Caribbean

BRITISH
SPANISH
UNITED STATES

Yet when Jefferson took office, Spain controlled all the land west of the Mississippi, as well as Florida.

Jefferson knew that as yet America could not challenge Spain for control of the whole territory. Eventually, he hoped, America would acquire it "piece by piece."

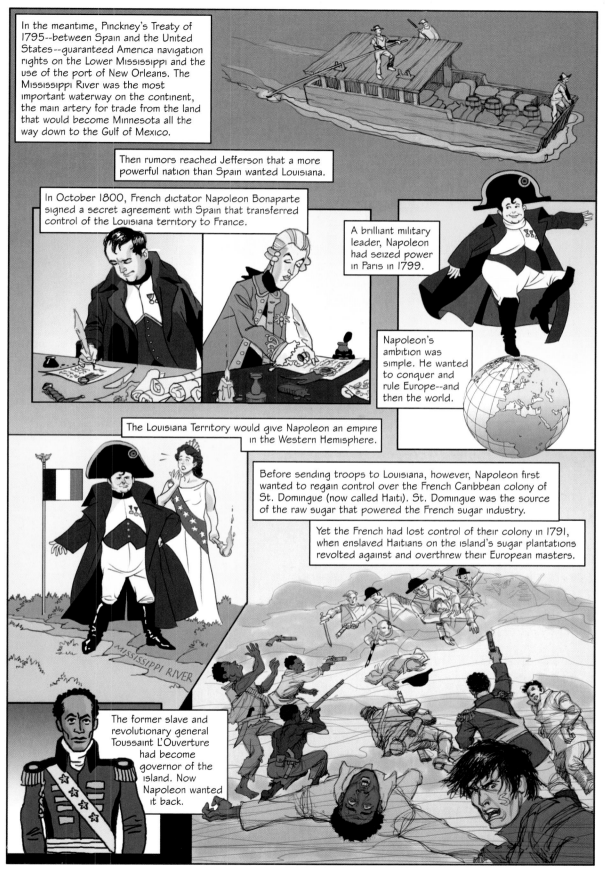

In the meantime, Pinckney's Treaty of 1795--between Spain and the United States--guaranteed America navigation rights on the Lower Mississippi and the use of the port of New Orleans. The Mississippi River was the most important waterway on the continent, the main artery for trade from the land that would become Minnesota all the way down to the Gulf of Mexico.

Then rumors reached Jefferson that a more powerful nation than Spain wanted Louisiana.

In October 1800, French dictator Napoleon Bonaparte signed a secret agreement with Spain that transferred control of the Louisiana territory to France.

A brilliant military leader, Napoleon had seized power in Paris in 1799.

Napoleon's ambition was simple. He wanted to conquer and rule Europe--and then the world.

The Louisiana Territory would give Napoleon an empire in the Western Hemisphere.

Before sending troops to Louisiana, however, Napoleon first wanted to regain control over the French Caribbean colony of St. Domingue (now called Haiti). St. Domingue was the source of the raw sugar that powered the French sugar industry.

Yet the French had lost control of their colony in 1791, when enslaved Haitians on the island's sugar plantations revolted against and overthrew their European masters.

MISSISSIPPI RIVER

The former slave and revolutionary general Toussaint L'Ouverture had become governor of the island. Now Napoleon wanted it back.

In February 1802, Napoleon dispatched an invasion force of 35,000 men to St. Domingue to defeat Toussaint's army and reinstate slavery.

The French captured Toussaint, but the fight continued.

Meanwhile, an alarmed Jefferson dispatched his old friend Robert Livingston to France to find out whether its treaty with Spain actually existed.

IF FRANCE *DOES* HAVE CONTROL OF NEW ORLEANS, FRANCE AND THE UNITED STATES CANNOT BE FRIENDS.

In France, Livingston met with Talleyrand, Napoleon's minister of foreign affairs, who lied to him.

I CAN ASSURE YOU, NO SUCH AGREEMENT HAS BEEN CONCLUDED.

MARCH 1802. But Livingston was not fooled. He wrote to Jefferson that his sources reported French troops were going to occupy Louisiana after they left St. Domingue.

Jefferson told Livingston that as soon as France sailed into New Orleans, the United States would ally itself with Britain. Jefferson trusted that Napoleon would heed this warning.

In May of 1802, Jefferson finally received proof that France now owned Louisiana ...

MY ORDERS ARE TO TAKE POSSESSION OF NEW ORLEANS. OFFICIALLY, OF COURSE, WE ARE MERELY GOING TO ST. DOMINGUE.

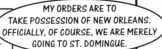

Meanwhile, Napoleon secretly assembled a fleet in Holland to invade North America. When Livingston suggested that France cede New Orleans to the United States, the French emperor ignored him.

November 1802. The departure of the French navy was repeatedly delayed, as was the transfer of New Orleans from Spain to France. Possibly at Napoleon's request, the Spanish closed warehouses in the port of New Orleans to U.S. goods, which were intended to be shipped to the East Coast and to Europe. He put a stranglehold on American commerce.

March 1803. Jefferson decided to send another envoy to Paris: the former Virginia governor James Monroe. He carried instructions to *offer to buy* New Orleans and Florida. If necessary, he and Livingston could offer as much as $10 million.

BUT IF NAPOLEON WILL NOT DEAL WITH US, WE MUST MAKE AN ALLIANCE WITH BRITAIN.

That spring, Napoleon also learned that his invasion of St. Domingue had ended in disaster. Fierce Haitian resistance--and deadly yellow fever--destroyed nearly all the French forces.

His dream of a European empire, however, had not. Napoleon badly needed money to finance his renewed war against the British and their allies.

I RENOUNCE LOUISIANA. IT IS NOT ONLY NEW ORLEANS THAT I WILL CEDE. IT IS THE WHOLE TERRITORY.

Napoleon had to face the fact that his hopes for an empire in the Western Hemisphere had vanished with his army.

April 11, 1803. Talleyrand summoned Livingston and made an amazing offer.

DO YOU WISH TO HAVE THE WHOLE OF LOUISIANA?

NO, WE NEED ONLY NEW ORLEANS AND THE FLORIDAS.

WHAT WOULD YOU GIVE FOR THE WHOLE OF IT?

WHAT?

Livingston realized that Napoleon was serious about selling all of the Louisiana Territory. The negotiations continued for the next few weeks.

France demanded $22 million . . .

and the United States offered $8 million.

France lowered its demand to $16 million . . .

and the United States raised its offer to $12 million.

Livingston and Monroe wrote to Secretary of State James Madison every day, keeping him informed of their negotiations. But their letters took eight weeks to cross the Atlantic Ocean--and replies took months longer.

WE CANNOT WAIT FOR OFFICIAL APPROVAL.

WE MUST ACT ON OUR OWN!

May 2, 1803. Livingston and Monroe signed the Louisiana Purchase Treaty with France.

SOLD! To the United States of America. All of the Louisiana Territory for $15 million. That's 829,000 acres, for about four cents an acre. Great deal!

When the news of the treaty reached President Jefferson on July 3, he was thrilled. Even though the U.S. government did not possess $15 million, two British and Dutch banks gave the new nation a loan. Britain wanted to keep France out of America at any cost.

But Jefferson also faced a dilemma. In his view, the Constitution did not authorize the president to purchase territory.

Then word reached Jefferson that Napoleon was reconsidering the deal. The president decided to ignore his qualms about constitutionality . . . and the Senate ratified the treaty within three days.

In the spring of 1804, Jefferson dispatched an expedition to explore Louisiana and beyond. He charged Lewis and Clark's Corps of Discovery with investigating the new territories, identifying new animals and plants, and befriending the Indians.

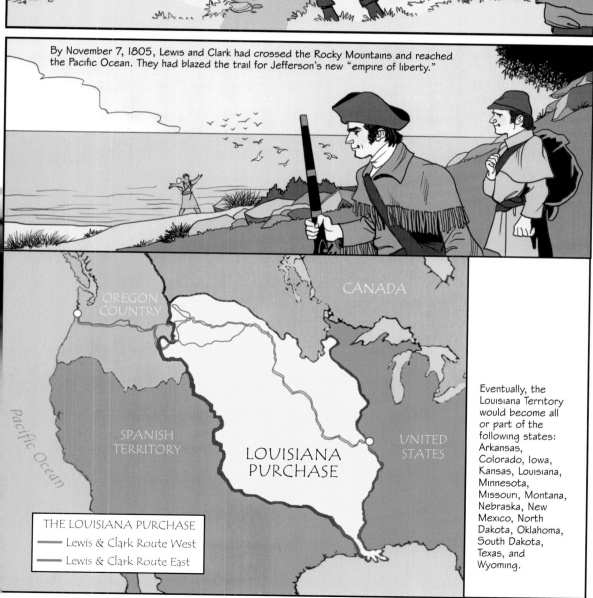

By November 7, 1805, Lewis and Clark had crossed the Rocky Mountains and reached the Pacific Ocean. They had blazed the trail for Jefferson's new "empire of liberty."

CANADA

OREGON COUNTRY

Pacific Ocean

SPANISH TERRITORY

LOUISIANA PURCHASE

UNITED STATES

THE LOUISIANA PURCHASE

— Lewis & Clark Route West
— Lewis & Clark Route East

Eventually, the Louisiana Territory would become all or part of the following states: Arkansas, Colorado, Iowa, Kansas, Louisiana, Minnesota, Missouri, Montana, Nebraska, New Mexico, North Dakota, Oklahoma, South Dakota, Texas, and Wyoming.

The Louisiana Purchase was both a stroke of luck and a triumph of international diplomacy. It opened the West for peaceful settlement, with no conflict with Spain or France. It also gave the United States a long-desired port--New Orleans--that was both at the mouth of the Mississippi River and an outlet to the Gulf of Mexico.

The purchase required Jefferson to compromise his belief in a less powerful executive office. Although the power to acquire territory is not spelled out in the Constitution, the unique opportunity to double the size of the nation required immediate and forceful action. In this case, Jefferson's cherished vision of American westward expansion prompted him to ignore abstract principle and act decisively in his nation's best interest.

EXCERPT FROM THE LOUISIANA PURCHASE TREATY

"The First Consul of the French Republic desiring to give to the United States a strong proof of his friendship doth hereby cede to the United States in the name of the French Republic for ever and in full Sovereignty the [Louisiana Territory] with all its rights and appurtenances as fully and in the Same manner as they have been acquired by the French Republic."

"The Star-Spangled Banner"

The ongoing Napoleonic Wars between France and Britain-- which lasted from 1799 to 1815--put the United States in a difficult position. Eventually, the new nation found itself drawn into the conflict. The resulting war with Britain--what some called the Second War of Independence--inspired a wave of patriotism and produced a rousing national anthem.

President Jefferson tried to maintain America's neutrality and avoid *entangling alliances*. Yet France and Britain continued to seize American ships that were trading with their respective enemies. In desperate need of manpower, Britain also captured about 6,000 American sailors, claiming they were British deserters, and forced them to work on British ships.

On June 23, 1807, the British warship HMS *Leopard* gave chase to the USS *Chesapeake* and demanded it turn over four "British" seamen. When the American captain refused, the *Leopard* fired on the *Chesapeake*.

The *Chesapeake* was forced to surrender.

The British seized the four men. Eventually, three were identified as Americans and released. The fourth was hanged as a deserter.

Many Americans, insulted and angry, demanded war. Jefferson and his secretary of state, James Madison, instead opted to place an embargo on American trade. American merchants were forbidden to trade with any foreign nation.

Jefferson hoped to harm British and French business and force both nations to respect American shipping.

MAKE HER FAST! THIS SHIP IS GOING NOWHERE.

But the plan backfired. The Embargo Act of 1807 crippled the American economy. Sailors lost their jobs; merchants went bankrupt; farmers could not sell their goods.

HAVE PITY, SIR, ON A SAILOR'S WIFE.

March 1809. Congress repealed the Embargo Act during Jefferson's last week in office. They replaced it with the Non-Intercourse Act, which outlawed trade with just Great Britain and France.

May 1810. When impressment persisted, the new president, James Madison, backed Macon's Bill Number 2. It temporarily restored trade with both Britain and France--but promised exclusive trade with the first nation to recognize American neutrality.

Napoleon sent word that he would stop attacking American ships. As a reward, President Madison promptly suspended trade with Britain.

The United States and Britain had taken a step closer to war.

Democratic-Republican "war hawks" in Congress were *eager* for war with Britain. They thought it would be the perfect opportunity to push the British from Canada and expand American territory.

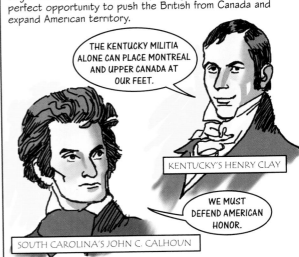

THE KENTUCKY MILITIA ALONE CAN PLACE MONTREAL AND UPPER CANADA AT OUR FEET.

KENTUCKY'S HENRY CLAY

WE MUST DEFEND AMERICAN HONOR.

SOUTH CAROLINA'S JOHN C. CALHOUN

Southerners and westerners also distrusted Britain because of its alliances with Indians in the western territories.

THE ONCE POWERFUL TRIBES OF OUR PEOPLE ARE VANISHING BEFORE THE OPPRESSION OF THE WHITE MAN.

The inspirational Shawnee chief Tecumseh wanted to unite all Indian tribes against the advance of white settlers.

THE ONLY WAY TO CHECK AND STOP ALL THIS EVIL IS FOR ALL RED MEN TO UNITE IN CLAIMING A COMMON AND EQUAL RIGHT IN THE LAND.

Indiana Territory, November 7, 1811.

Tecumseh and his brother, the prophet Tenskwatawa, founded a community of many different tribes, called Prophetstown. But in a battle with the Indiana militia and its Indian allies, Prophetstown was burned and the community destroyed.

The discovery that Tecumseh's warriors were using British weapons aided the cause of the American war hawks.

June 18, 1812. President Madison finally gave in to the pressure and signed a declaration of war against Britain, although the British navy boasted 600 ships compared with the Americans' 16.

Nonetheless, many of America's victories were at sea. On August 19, 1812, the USS *Constitution* won its battle against the HMS *Guerriere*. Other naval triumphs followed. The United States benefited from the fact that most of Britain's fleet and armies were trying to defeat Napoleon in Europe.

Americans expected immediate success against the British in Canada.

THE ACQUISITION OF CANADA THIS YEAR WILL BE A MERE MATTER OF MARCHING.

But it turned out that Canadians did not want to be citizens of a new American state. American troops lost Detroit on August 16, 1812. The next year, when they invaded York, Ontario--now Toronto--they put much of the town to the torch.

The British rear admiral George Cockburn vowed retaliation.

WE WILL GO TO WASHINGTON AND BURN DOWN THE PRESIDENT'S HOUSE!

October 1813.

The American general William Henry Harrison retook Detroit. Tecumseh, fighting as a brigadier general on the side of the British, died during the battles on the Canadian border. With him died the hopes for Indian unity.

The British had not brought the war to the shores of the United States. That changed in April 1814, when Napoleon suffered defeat in Europe and surrendered. The vast British war machine turned its attention to the United States.

August 1814. The British landed in Maryland and, as Cockburn had threatened, began to march toward the capital city of Washington.

August 22, 1814. President Madison departed Washington to be with his ill-prepared army at the front. The Americans met the British at Bladensburg, Maryland, and were routed in a quick battle.

Madison's wife, Dolley, was left behind to pack up the President's House . . .

I HAVE PRESSED AS MANY CABINET PAPERS INTO TRUNKS AS TO FILL A CARRIAGE . . . I AM DETERMINED NOT TO GO MYSELF UNTIL I SEE MR. MADISON SAFE.

August 24, 1814. Time was running out.

CLEAR OUT! THE BRITISH ARE COMING!

I SHALL NOT LEAVE WITHOUT MR. WASHINGTON'S PAINTING.

Saving what she could, Dolley Madison jumped into her carriage and sped off into the Virginia countryside. Within hours, the British marched into the city.

By nine o'clock that night, they were in the House of Representatives. Rear Admiral George Cockburn perched himself in the Speaker's chair and called for a mock vote.

SHALL THIS HARBOR OF AMERICAN DEMOCRACY BE BURNED? ALL FOR IT SAY AYE!

AYE!

The Capitol went up in flames. Then it was on to the President's House, where Cockburn toasted "Jemmy Madison" with the president's best wine and ordered the building torched.

The British also burned the Treasury, the Library of Congress, and other public buildings to the ground. Having gotten their revenge for York, they turned around and marched back to their ships.

The British had invaded the capital of the United States with virtually no opposition.

Yet America's humiliation at the hands of the British only strengthened its citizens' resolve.

WE WILL REBUILD, MY DEAR.*

The next British attack would come in Baltimore, then the nation's third-largest city. Its harbor was defended by the star-shaped Fort McHenry and a thousand American troops.

Above the fort waved an enormous flag, recently commissioned from a Baltimore seamstress. Thirty feet high and 42 feet long, it was visible from a great distance.

* The President's House was rebuilt, and its reddish stone was whitewashed, becoming what today is known as the White House.

September 13, 1814. British warships began their bombardment of Fort McHenry at seven o'clock in the morning. The assault would last for 25 hours.

One fascinated observer was the young American lawyer Francis Scott Key, who watched the battle from a British ship a short distance away. He had come aboard on a mission to obtain the release of a captured American doctor but was not allowed to leave until the attack was over.

The shelling continued all day and into the night. As dawn broke, Key peered into the distance.

IS THAT THE *BRITISH* FLAG FLYING OVER THE FORT?

No, it was the Stars and Stripes! The British had not taken the fort after all! Overjoyed, Key began to write a celebratory poem on the back of an old letter.

"O say can you see, by the dawn's early light,
What so proudly we hailed at the twilight's last gleaming,
Whose broad stripes and bright stars, through the perilous fight,
O'er the ramparts we watched were so gallantly streaming?

September 14. Despite their overwhelming firepower, the British could not destroy the fort or defeat its defenders. They abandoned their assault and departed. The war was not over, but Baltimore--and the whole eastern shore of the young nation--were saved from British occupation.

Key recalled the spectacular barrage of the night before. In one rocket flash, he had seen that an American flag was still flying.

"And the rocket's red glare, the bombs bursting in air, / Gave proof through the night that our flag was still there...

O SAY CAN YOU SEE, BY THE DAWN'S EARLY LIGHT...

By that afternoon, Key was back in Baltimore, where he scribbled down the rest of the poem and rushed it to a printer. Within days, the poem had circulated throughout the town and been turned into a rousing anthem, sung to the tune of an old drinking song, "To Anacreon in Heaven."

The song quickly became a national sensation, making its way to New Orleans, where a military band played it to General Andrew Jackson.

January 8, 1815. It was Jackson who had led the American troops in the Battle of New Orleans, the largest conflict of the War of 1812.

In an astounding victory, Jackson's force destroyed an army twice its size. The British lost 2,057; the Americans, just 13.

December 24, 1814, Treaty of Ghent.

Ironically, by the time that battle was fought, the United States had already signed a peace treaty with Britain, though no one in America knew it because it took months for the signed treaty to be shipped across the Atlantic. In one sense, the war changed nothing--the relationship between Britain and the United States went back to what it had been before the war.

But in another, everything had changed. For the second time, the United States had taken on the mightiest nation on earth . . . and proved itself.

WE OWE ALLEGIANCE TO NO CROWN

A spirit of nationalism swept the country, and the symbol of that feeling was immortalized in a passionately patriotic song. Francis Scott Key's "Star-Spangled Banner" officially became the American national anthem on March 3, 1931.

The anthem captures the tenacity of the Americans resisting the British invasion. Francis Scott Key, an eyewitness to the bombing of Baltimore's Fort McHenry in 1814, expressed the exuberant patriotism of Americans then and today.

EXCERPT FROM
"THE STAR-SPANGLED BANNER"

O say can you see, by the dawn's early light,

What so proudly we hailed at the twilight's last gleaming,

Whose broad stripes and bright stars through the perilous fight,

O'er the ramparts we watched were so gallantly streaming?

And the rocket's red glare, the bombs bursting in air,

Gave proof through the night that our flag was still there,

O say does that star-spangled banner yet wave

O'er the land of the free and the home of the brave?

On the shore dimly seen through the mists of the deep

Where the foe's haughty host in dread silence reposes,

What is that which the breeze, o'er the towering steep,

As it fitfully blows, half conceals, half discloses?

Now it catches the gleam of the morning's first beam,

In full glory reflected now shines in the stream,

'Tis the star-spangled banner! O long may it wave

O'er the land of the free and the home of the brave!

The Missouri Compromise

The Louisiana Purchase opened up a huge area of land to American exploration and settlement. But when the time came for these territories to apply for statehood, the United States was faced with a dilemma: Should the territories be admitted as slave states or free states? The storm that erupted when Missouri became a state in 1820 forecast conflict in the years to come between those who favored slavery and those who did not.

From New York and Pennsylvania, from Virginia and Maryland, the settlers came. They moved westward over the Appalachian Mountains to the fertile lands beyond. They traveled by Conestoga wagons and on flatboats, by land, by river, and by foot, bringing with them their children, oxen, axes, and Bibles--and sometimes their slaves.

Whether settlers brought their own slaves into slave-owning areas or moved into free territories often depended on their own background. For instance, in 1797, Henry Clay, an ambitious young lawyer from Virginia, traveled the Wilderness Road into Kentucky . . .

. . . to rejoin his remarried mother and her family, who had migrated a few years earlier. The first thing his stepfather did was give Clay back his "property."

YOUR FATHER LEFT YOU LITTLE SAM IN HIS WILL.

As a young man, Clay supported the gradual emancipation of slaves. But he would also own slaves his whole life.

Abraham Lincoln's ancestors had moved steadily westward, from England, to Massachusetts, Pennsylvania, Virginia, and then to Kentucky, where Abraham was born in 1809.

Abraham's mother and father had religious objections to slavery. So when Abraham was seven, they moved from slave-owning Kentucky to the free state of Indiana, where slavery was outlawed.

Slavery was thriving in much of the United States in the first decades of the 19th century. At the time of the Constitutional Convention, most of the Founding Fathers, even the slaveholders, would have been surprised by this development. They had expected slavery to gradually disappear over time.

THERE IS NOT A MAN LIVING WHO WISHES MORE SINCERELY THAN I DO TO SEE A PLAN ADOPTED FOR THE ABOLITION OF IT.

SLAVERY IS THE MOST OPPRESSIVE DOMINATION EVER EXERCISED BY MAN OVER MAN.

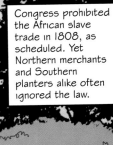

Congress prohibited the African slave trade in 1808, as scheduled. Yet Northern merchants and Southern planters alike often ignored the law.

ABOLITION
Vermont 1777
Maine 1780
Massachusetts 1780
New Hampshire 1783

GRADUAL EMANCIPATION COMPLETED
New York 1827
New Jersey 1846
Pennsylvania 1847
Connecticut 1848

Nonetheless, in the Northern states, legal slavery began to vanish as state legislatures passed laws to abolish it or gradually phase it out.

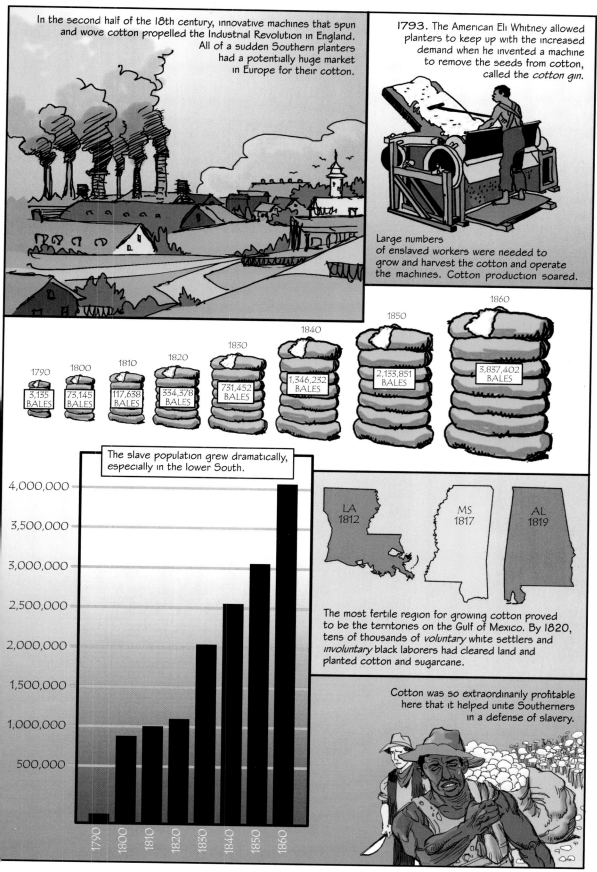

In the second half of the 18th century, innovative machines that spun and wove cotton propelled the Industrial Revolution in England. All of a sudden Southern planters had a potentially huge market in Europe for their cotton.

1793. The American Eli Whitney allowed planters to keep up with the increased demand when he invented a machine to remove the seeds from cotton, called the *cotton gin*.

Large numbers of enslaved workers were needed to grow and harvest the cotton and operate the machines. Cotton production soared.

1790 — 3,135 BALES
1800 — 73,145 BALES
1810 — 117,638 BALES
1820 — 334,378 BALES
1830 — 731,452 BALES
1840 — 1,346,232 BALES
1850 — 2,133,851 BALES
1860 — 3,837,402 BALES

The slave population grew dramatically, especially in the lower South.

4,000,000
3,500,000
3,000,000
2,500,000
2,000,000
1,500,000
1,000,000
500,000

1790 1800 1810 1820 1830 1840 1850 1860

LA 1812   MS 1817   AL 1819

The most fertile region for growing cotton proved to be the territories on the Gulf of Mexico. By 1820, tens of thousands of *voluntary* white settlers and *involuntary* black laborers had cleared land and planted cotton and sugarcane.

Cotton was so extraordinarily profitable here that it helped unite Southerners in a defense of slavery.

In the early 1800s, different regions of the country developed their own economies and ways of life. Factory workers in the New England and Mid-Atlantic states produced textiles, machinery, and other goods for the country . . .

. . . whereas planters dependent on slave labor dominated the economy of the South.

And in the West, independent farmers worked fields of wheat and corn, shipping their produce down the Mississippi River to market.

The most important difference between the states is that some allowed slavery and some did not. By 1819, there were 11 slave states and 11 free states. This meant that each group had 22 senators in the U.S. Senate, or 2 from each state.

But the more populous free states had the majority of representatives in the House.

Slave States

Free States

Then the territory of Missouri applied for statehood.

MISSOURI

Slave States

Free States

Most Missouri settlers had come from the slave-owning states Kentucky and Tennessee. Already, 15 percent of Missouri's population was enslaved people.

February 13, 1819.

The New York congressman James Tallmadge took the floor of the House of Representatives with a startling amendment to the Missouri statehood bill.

NEW SLAVES SHOULD BE *PROHIBITED* FROM ENTERING THE STATE OF MISSOURI. SLAVE CHILDREN BORN IN THE STATE AFTER ADMISSION SHOULD BE FREED AT AGE 25.

Debates ignited by Tallmadge's proposal raged in Congress--and throughout the country. These debates were repeated for the next 40 years, reflecting deep sectional divides.

SLAVE STATES' ARGUMENTS

RESTRICTING SLAVERY IS AN EXAMPLE OF FEDERAL TYRANNY!

States' Rights

John Randolph, Virginia

MISSOURI CITIZENS MUST DECIDE THE SLAVERY QUESTION FOR THEMSELVES.

John Scott, Missouri

Economic

OUR SLAVES ARE WORTH AT LEAST $600 MILLION. THE LOSS OF THEM AND OF THE LANDS THEY CULTIVATE WOULD BE FELT BY THE WHOLE UNION.

Charles Pinckney, South Carolina

Slavery Is Benevolent

THE GREAT BODY OF SLAVES ARE HAPPIER IN THEIR PRESENT SITUATION THAN THEY COULD BE IN ANY OTHER.

William Pinkney, Maryland

Religious Authority

GOD UPHELD SLAVERY IN THE BIBLE.

William Smith, South Carolina

FREE STATES' ARGUMENTS

Nationalism

STATES' RIGHTS SHOULD BE SECONDARY TO THE COMMON DEFENSE, THE GENERAL WELFARE, AND THE WISE ADMINISTRATION OF GOVERNMENT THROUGHOUT THE WHOLE UNION.

Rufus King, New York

Slavery in New States Unconstitutional

NORTHWEST TERRITORY 1800

CANADA

Wisconsin

Michigan

LOUISIANA TERRITORY

Illinois   Indiana   Ohio

UNITED STATES

THE FOUNDING FATHERS HAD TAKEN STEPS TOWARD EVENTUAL ABOLITION IN THE ORIGINAL STATES AND PROHIBITED SLAVERY IN THE NORTHWEST TERRITORY.

William Plumer Jr., New Hampshire

Natural Rights

SLAVERY CONTRADICTS THE PRINCIPLES OF EQUALITY IN THE DECLARATION OF INDEPENDENCE.

John W. Taylor, New York

Morality

IT IS THE RIGHT AND DUTY OF CONGRESS TO HALT THE INTOLERABLE EVIL OF SLAVERY.

Timothy Fuller, Massachusetts

As expected, the House--with its majority of free-state members--passed the Tallmadge Amendment prohibiting new slaves in Missouri. But the Senate rejected it.

When Congress met again the following December, there was a new development: the northeast territory of Maine had also applied for statehood. Speaker of the House Henry Clay had an idea.

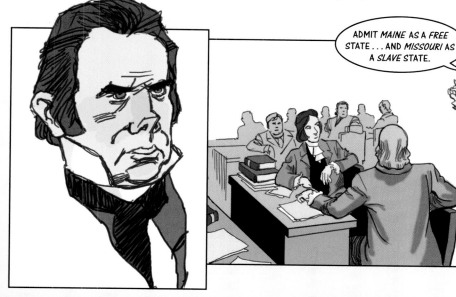

ADMIT *MAINE* AS A *FREE* STATE... AND *MISSOURI* AS A *SLAVE* STATE.

That way, the balance would be maintained.

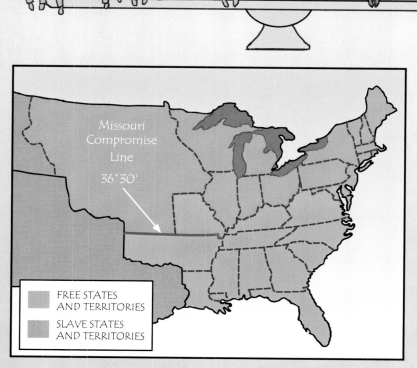

Missouri Compromise Line 36°30'

FREE STATES AND TERRITORIES

SLAVE STATES AND TERRITORIES

The Illinois senator Jesse Thomas proposed what came to be known as the Missouri Compromise. Maine and Missouri would be admitted at the same time. In addition, all states formed from the Louisiana Territory above latitude 36°30' would be free. Those below the line would be able to *choose* whether or not to allow slavery.

March 6, 1820. Under the congressional leadership of Henry Clay, the Missouri Compromise was passed and signed into law.

Yet Clay, an avid nationalist, was not happy about the deepening sectional disagreements. He expressed his fears to Secretary of State John Quincy Adams.

I PREDICT THAT WITHIN FIVE YEARS OUR NATION WILL COME APART TO FORM THREE REPRESENTATIONAL CONFEDERACIES.

The controversy also made the elderly Thomas Jefferson worry for the future of his nation. As a slave owner himself, he understood why Southern whites depended on the slave economy. But how could the nation reconcile slavery with the ideal of liberty?

"THIS MOMENTOUS QUESTION, LIKE A FIRE BELL IN THE NIGHT, AWAKENED AND FILLED ME WITH TERROR. I CONSIDERED IT AT ONCE AS THE KNELL OF THE UNION."

Jefferson compared the nation's dilemma to that of a man who has caught a vicious animal: "As it is, we have the wolf by the ear, and we can neither hold him, nor safely let him go."

Such fears would prove prophetic. But in 1820, the Missouri Compromise allowed the nation to temporarily put aside the problem of slavery and get on with the business of creating wealth and spreading democracy.

The Missouri Compromise was a legislative victory that maintained the balance between slave states and free states in 1820. It also attempted to determine the future status of slavery in states that would join the Union in the future.

However, the compromise was only a temporary solution to the contentious slavery issue. By exposing disagreements between Northern free states and Southern slave states, it ushered in an age of sectionalism.

EXCERPTS FROM THE MISSOURI COMPROMISE

"*Be it enacted by the Senate and House of Representatives of the United States of America, in Congress assembled,* That the inhabitants of that portion of the Missouri territory included within the boundaries hereinafter designated, be, and they are hereby, authorized to form for themselves a constitution and state government . . .

"*And be it further enacted,* That in all that territory ceded by France to the United States, under the name of Louisiana, which lies north of thirty-six degrees and thirty minutes north latitude, not included within the limits of the state, contemplated by this act, slavery and involuntary servitude . . . shall be, and is hereby, forever prohibited."

March 6, 1820

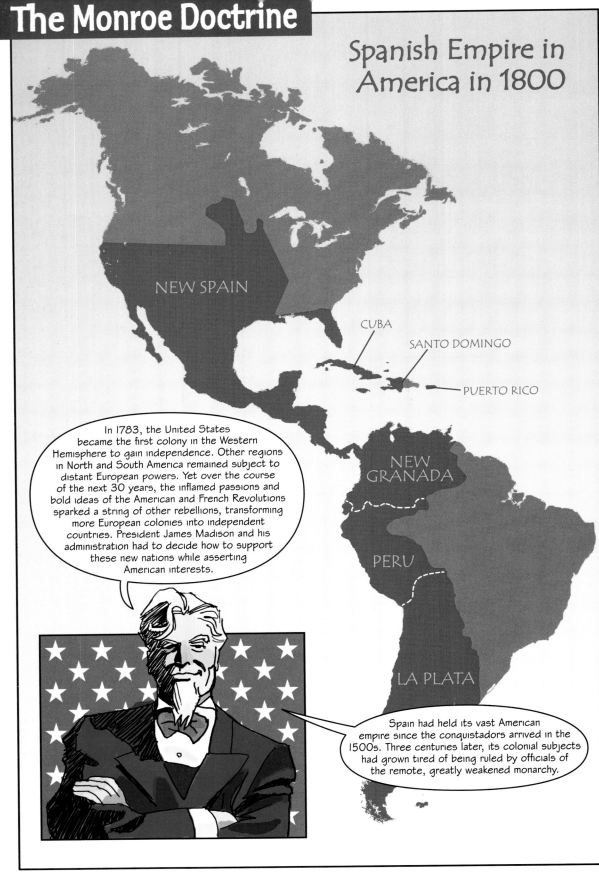

The Monroe Doctrine

Spanish Empire in America in 1800

NEW SPAIN

CUBA

SANTO DOMINGO

PUERTO RICO

NEW GRANADA

PERU

LA PLATA

In 1783, the United States became the first colony in the Western Hemisphere to gain independence. Other regions in North and South America remained subject to distant European powers. Yet over the course of the next 30 years, the inflamed passions and bold ideas of the American and French Revolutions sparked a string of other rebellions, transforming more European colonies into independent countries. President James Madison and his administration had to decide how to support these new nations while asserting American interests.

Spain had held its vast American empire since the conquistadors arrived in the 1500s. Three centuries later, its colonial subjects had grown tired of being ruled by officials of the remote, greatly weakened monarchy.

Simón Bolívar, a wealthy Venezuelan who would become known as the Liberator, dedicated himself to the cause of independence when he was still a young man.

I SWEAR TO YOU, BY THE GOD OF MY FATHERS AND THE HONOR OF THE COUNTRY, I WILL NOT REST, NOT IN BODY OR SOUL, TILL I HAVE BROKEN THE CHAINS OF SPAIN.

In the early 1800s, all of Europe was embroiled in the Napoleonic Wars. When Napoleon's armies invaded Spain and overthrew the king, Bolívar saw his opportunity.

July 5, 1811. While Spain was engulfed by turmoil, Venezuela declared independence.

Spain did not easily relinquish power over its colonies. The extraordinarily brutal wars that followed Venezuela's declaration raged on and off for more than a decade. Yet by 1823, Bolívar and his armies had liberated not only Venezuela but also Colombia, Ecuador, Bolivia, and Panama.

The Argentinian revolutionary José de San Martín also freed Argentina from Spanish rule and crossed the Andes to defeat Spain in Chile and Peru.

Spanish Mexico fell to revolutionaries in 1821, after a war of independence that had lasted 10 years.

Many in the United States sympathized with the goals of the Latin American revolutionaries, including Thomas Jefferson.

ANOTHER EXAMPLE OF MAN RISING IN HIS MIGHT AND BURSTING THE CHAINS OF HIS OPPRESSOR!

In addition, the United States had border problems with Spanish Florida. Seminole Indians regularly raided Georgia settlements, while fugitive slaves found sanctuary in Indian communities.

President Monroe deputized the hero of the War of 1812, General Andrew Jackson, to subdue the Seminoles and their black allies. In 1819, Jackson burned Seminole villages and killed or captured the inhabitants.

He also captured Spanish forts-- without the permission of the U.S. government. The Spanish broke off talks about Florida with the Monroe administration . . .

. . . but Secretary of State John Quincy Adams blamed the violence on the Spanish and the Indians. He put his case to the Spanish foreign minister, Luis de Onís.

IF SPAIN CANNOT GOVERN FLORIDA PROPERLY, IT MUST GIVE IT TO THE UNITED STATES.

In a triumph of diplomacy, in 1819 Adams successfully negotiated the Adams-Onís Treaty, in which Spain ceded Florida to the United States.

Its business with Spain concluded, in 1822 the United States felt free to grant formal diplomatic recognition to the new Latin American nations.

COLOMBIA

ARGENTINA

MEXICO

Spain seethed at the loss of its colonial empire. So did the old monarchies of Europe, which were alarmed by the spread of revolution. After the defeat of Napoleon in 1815, Austria, Russia, and Prussia, and then France, formed a "Holy Alliance" dedicated to the restoration of the old order. It seemed possible they would unite with Spain to win back its former possessions.

AUSTRIA

FRANCE

RUSSIA

PRUSSIA

The American government viewed Europe's diplomatic dance with alarm.

Monroe felt further pressured by Russian claims on the Pacific coast of North America, where the United States and Britain were already trade competitors. Now Russia demanded a trading monopoly from Russian Alaska down to Oregon Country.

July 1823. Secretary of State Adams informed the Russian ambassador that . . .

THE AMERICAN CONTINENTS ARE NO LONGER SUBJECTS FOR ANY NEW EUROPEAN COLONIAL ESTABLISHMENT.

August 1823. The United States found an ally in Great Britain, which wanted no interference in its trade with the new South American nations.

"SPAIN'S DESIRE TO REGAIN ITS FORMER COLONIES IS HOPELESS. SHALL WE JOINTLY DECLARE OUR OPPOSITION TO NEW TERRITORIAL CONQUEST?"

"WE HAVE ALREADY RECOGNIZED THE NEW SOUTH AMERICAN COUNTRIES. WILL YOU DO THE SAME?"

George Canning, British Foreign Secretary

Richard Rush, U.S. Minister to Great Britain

The United States knew that the power of the formidable British navy, the greatest in the world, would act as a deterrent to any attempt by the Holy Alliance to invade South America.

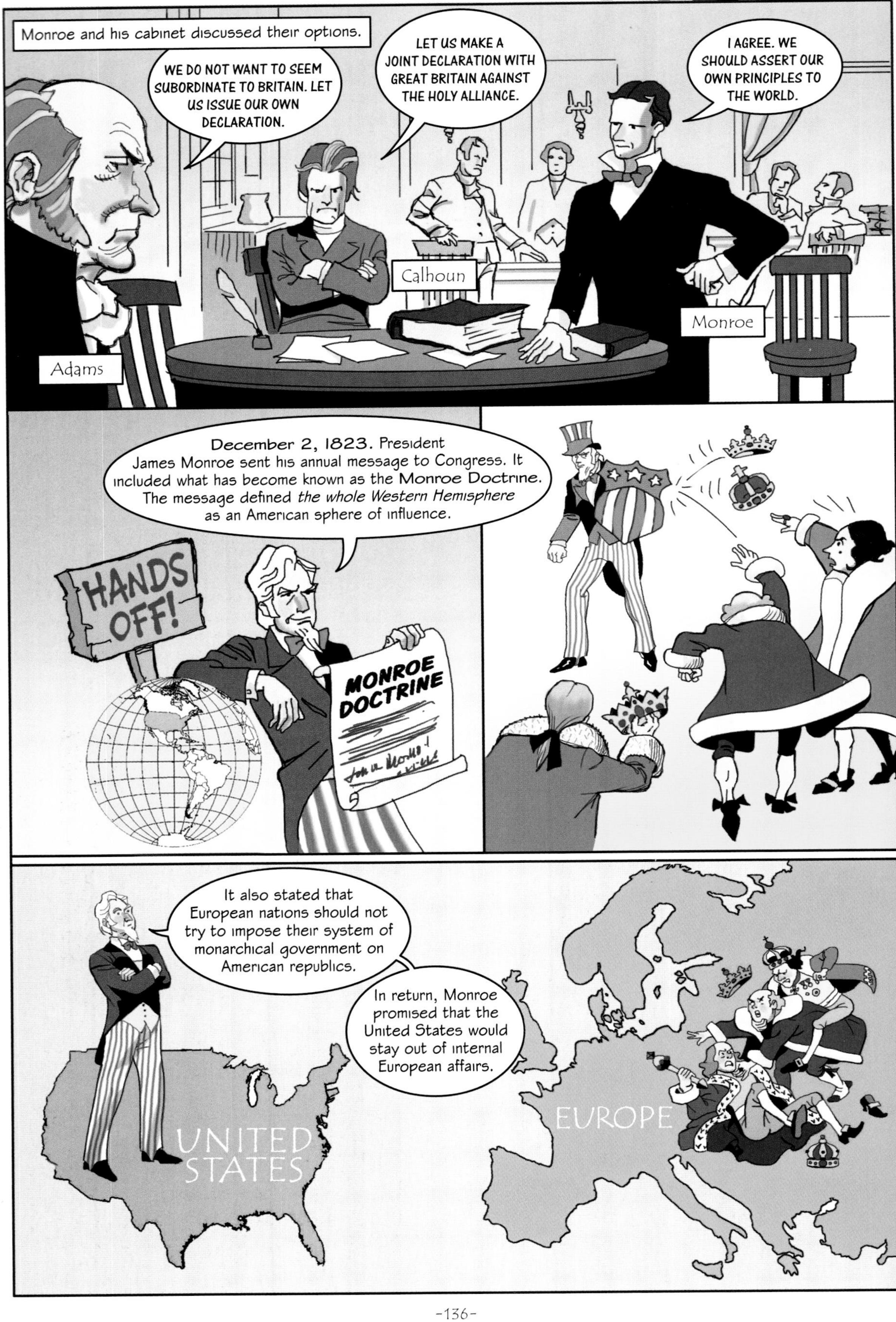

Monroe and his cabinet discussed their options.
WE DO NOT WANT TO SEEM SUBORDINATE TO BRITAIN. LET US ISSUE OUR OWN DECLARATION.
LET US MAKE A JOINT DECLARATION WITH GREAT BRITAIN AGAINST THE HOLY ALLIANCE.
I AGREE. WE SHOULD ASSERT OUR OWN PRINCIPLES TO THE WORLD.
Adams
Calhoun
Monroe
December 2, 1823. President James Monroe sent his annual message to Congress. It included what has become known as the Monroe Doctrine. The message defined *the whole Western Hemisphere* as an American sphere of influence.
HANDS OFF!
MONROE DOCTRINE
It also stated that European nations should not try to impose their system of monarchical government on American republics.
In return, Monroe promised that the United States would stay out of internal European affairs.
UNITED STATES
EUROPE

The Monroe Doctrine was a major development in U.S. foreign policy. It proclaimed the independence of American nations from European dominance and warned European nations not to try to influence systems of government anywhere in the Western Hemisphere. It also served as an expression of American nationalism in the wake of the War of 1812. Ever since, U.S. presidents have invoked the Monroe Doctrine to justify American protection of Latin American countries . . . as well as periodic interventions in Latin American politics.

EXCERPTS FROM THE MONROE DOCTRINE

"The American continents, by the free and independent condition which they have assumed and maintain, are henceforth not to be considered as subjects for future colonization by any European powers . . .

"We owe it . . . to the amicable relations existing between the United States and those powers to declare that we should consider any attempt on their part to extend their system to any portion of this hemisphere as dangerous to our peace and safety."

The Monroe Doctrine also assured Europe that the United States would continue Washington's and Jefferson's policy of noninterference in European affairs.

"Our policy in regard to Europe, which was adopted at an early stage of the wars which have so long agitated that quarter of the globe, nevertheless remains the same, which is, not to interfere in the internal concerns of any of its powers."

The Indian Removal Act

By the early 1800s, European and American settlement and expansion had reduced or annihilated most Native American tribes east of the Mississippi. The largest remaining populations were the Cherokee, Choctaw, Chickasaw, Creek, and Seminole. Known to the government and the settlers as the Five Civilized Tribes, they clung to what remained of their tribal lands in the Southeast. In 1830, the Indian Removal Act would uproot even these people and send them on a harrowing journey that would end with what is known as the Trail of Tears.

Georgia, May 1838. Sudden as the wind, U.S. Army troops swept onto Cherokee territory in Georgia and forced all residents to leave their farms and villages immediately. Within a month, more than 17,000 Cherokee had been rounded up, to be driven west across the Mississippi.

The Cherokee's desperate fight to save their homeland had been lost.

Long before Europeans first made contact with them in the 1500s, the Cherokee had lived in the lush, fertile lands of what are now North and South Carolina, Georgia, Alabama, Tennessee, and Kentucky.

Over the next two centuries, as other, more coastal Native peoples were destroyed by European settlement, the Cherokee, living farther inland, survived. Still, by 1700 they had lost half their land and half their people to land-hungry settlers, disease, and war.

All the tribes of the Southeast felt constant pressure from American pioneers who crossed the Appalachians in search of suitable land.

The first presidents of the United States wished to maintain peace with the southeastern tribes. Both George Washington and Thomas Jefferson encouraged them to become more like white people.

If all else failed, Jefferson thought, the tribes could be removed to the vast territory of the Louisiana Purchase.

Many Indians, particularly Cherokee, accepted government-issued farming tools and settled down.

The rise of the Cotton Kingdom in the first decades of the 1800s increased Americans' desire for the rich soil of the Southern frontier, which only increased their greed for Indian land. In a series of treaties between the U.S. government and the tribes, the Indians gave up millions of acres to planters.

Loss of Cherokee Territory
1500–1838
1500 1783 1838

The Cherokee sped up their attempt to prove they could be law-abiding citizens of their own nation. The most prosperous sent their children to missionary schools, where they learned English and Christianity. Like their Southern neighbors, they owned farms and farm animals, stores and mills-- and sometimes black slaves.

They even had their own written language and newspaper. In the 1820s, a brilliant ex-warrior named Sequoyah invented a sign for every syllable in the Cherokee language.

1827.
But when the Cherokee wrote a constitution modeled on that of the United States and declared themselves a sovereign nation, Georgians were furious. They soon passed a law that declared the Cherokee constitution null and void and made the Cherokee subject to state laws. Then gold was discovered in the state, and Cherokee land became even more desirable.

In 1828, Andrew Jackson was elected president of the United States. An old Indian fighter, Jackson was hostile to Native Americans. He shared the prevalent belief of the time that they were an inferior people.

"THEY HAVE NEITHER THE INTELLIGENCE, THE INDUSTRY, NOR THE DESIRE FOR IMPROVEMENT. ESTABLISHED IN THE MIDST OF ANOTHER AND SUPERIOR RACE, THEY MUST NECESSARILY YIELD."

He also believed that the *only* solution to the "Indian dilemma" was to relocate them all to a separate territory beyond the Mississippi River. In his mind, removal would benefit both white settlers and Indian tribes, who would not be killed in battles over land.

On December 8, 1829, Jackson proposed the Indian Removal Act to Congress.

To his surprise, protests erupted, mostly from Northern religious and reform groups.

THE LADIES OF STEUBENVILLE, OHIO, ARE SENDING CONGRESS A PETITION TO PROTEST INDIAN REMOVAL. WOULD YOU CARE TO SIGN?

I WOULD BE HAPPY TO.

Spring 1830. After heated debate, Congress passed the Indian Removal Act.

WE CALL THEM BROTHERS . . . BUT *STEAL* THEIR LAND.

It authorized the president to make treaties that exchanged tribal land in the East for land west of the Mississippi River. New Jersey's senator Theodore Frelinghuysen was among the northern politicians who felt the terms were disgraceful.

Between 1830 and 1837, Indian tribes were tricked, bribed, and intimidated into signing treaties with the U.S. government. Despite resistance, the Choctaw, Chickasaw, and Creek were forced west to Indian Territory (present-day Oklahoma). The Seminole waged a guerrilla war against the United States for years before being defeated.

WE ARE FAR FROM OUR HOMELAND.

The French visitor Alexis de Tocqueville witnessed the Chocktaw's forced winter crossing of the Mississippi: "There were among them the wounded, the sick, newborn babies, and the old men on the point of death . . . Neither sob nor complaint rose from that silent assembly. Their afflictions were of long standing."

The Cherokee, though, decided to resist removal by fighting a series of legal battles.

Bill of Rights

They were confident that under the First Amendment they could petition the government for redress of grievances.

Chief John Ross hired a famous lawyer to challenge Georgia's refusal to recognize the Cherokee Nation.

AS OUR LAWYER, YOU SHOULD UPHOLD OUR RIGHT AS AN INDEPENDENT NATION TO KEEP OUR LAND.

The lawyer William Wirt challenged Georgia law in the Supreme Court. In both *Cherokee Nation* v. *Georgia* and *Worcester* v. *Georgia*, Chief Justice John Marshall affirmed that the Cherokee were a dependent nation under the authority of the United States. They were not subject to state laws.

THE CHEROKEE NATION IS A DISTINCT COMMUNITY, OCCUPYING ITS OWN TERRITORY . . . IN WHICH THE LAWS OF GEORGIA CAN HAVE NO FORCE . . . THE ACTS OF GEORGIA ARE REPUGNANT TO THE CONSTITUTION, LAWS, AND TREATIES OF THE UNITED STATES.

But Jackson had no intention of halting the removal of Indians from Georgia and defied the Supreme Court ruling.

JOHN MARSHALL HAS MADE HIS DECISION. NOW LET HIM ENFORCE IT.

Bill of Rights

The governor of Georgia sneered that his state "is not accountable to the Supreme Court or any other tribunal on earth." Georgia held a lottery and sold off Cherokee land.

THIS IS MY PROPERTY NOW. GET OUT!

1836. Chief John Ross tried to bargain with Jackson, but the president refused his offer. Instead, Jackson made a deal with a small group of men who did not represent most of the Cherokee. By signing the Treaty of New Echota, leaders such as Major Ridge hoped they were saving the lives of their people. But they feared for their own.

WITH THIS TREATY, I SIGN MY DEATH WARRANT.

The Cherokee later assassinated the signers for selling off tribal land.

Sixteen thousand Cherokee signed a petition against the treaty and sent it to Congress. But despite removal opponents such as Congressmen Henry Clay and John Quincy Adams, the treaty passed. President Jackson signed it on May 23, 1836.

The Cherokee were given two years to get out. Adams responded angrily . . .

THIS TREATY WILL BRING ETERNAL DISGRACE UPON THE COUNTRY!

In 1837, Chief Ross went to Washington to lobby the new president, Martin Van Buren.

GET THE INDIANS OUT OF GEORGIA, SIR!

Annoyed by the delay, Georgia threatened violence against the Indians. Van Buren gave orders to General Winfield Scott.

May 1838. Scott and most of the U.S. Army descended on northern Georgia and dragged women and children from their homes and men from the fields. People were given only a few minutes to grab a few belongings before being driven into crowded, disease-ridden stockades.

The roundup signaled open season on Cherokee land. White squatters looted anything they could find.

When the forced marches began, summer heat and drought killed many hundreds of Cherokee.

On October 1, 1838, the main convoy started on the 1,000-mile trek.

The army private John Burnett later wrote, "One can never forget the sadness and solemnity of that morning. When the bugle sounded and the wagons started rolling, many of the children waved their little hands good-bye to their mountain homes."

As fall turned to winter, people perished by the thousands from disease, exhaustion, and exposure. By the time they reached the designated Indian Territory, more than 4,000 Cherokee had died on Nunna dual Tsunyi--"the Trail Where We Cried."

Today we call it the Trail of Tears.

Sac & Fox
Chickasaw and Choctaw
Cherokee
Creek
Seminole

TRAIL OF TEARS
OTHER INDIAN REMOVALS
INDIAN RESERVATIONS

The Indian Removal Act forced more than 70,000 Native Americans from their ancestral homelands to reservations in the West. Andrew Jackson's policy marked a sharp departure from Jefferson's "civilizing" program of nearly 30 years before. To a great extent, the North/South divide over Indian removal mirrored the sectional disagreements on slavery and states' rights that would lead to the Civil War.

EXCERPT FROM THE
INDIAN REMOVAL ACT

"That it shall . . . be lawful for the President of the United States to cause so much of any territory belonging to the United States, west of the river Mississippi . . . to be divided into a suitable number of districts, for the reception of such tribes or nations of Indians as may choose to exchange the lands where they now reside, and remove there; and to cause each of said districts to be so described by natural or artificial marks, as to be easily distinguished from every other."

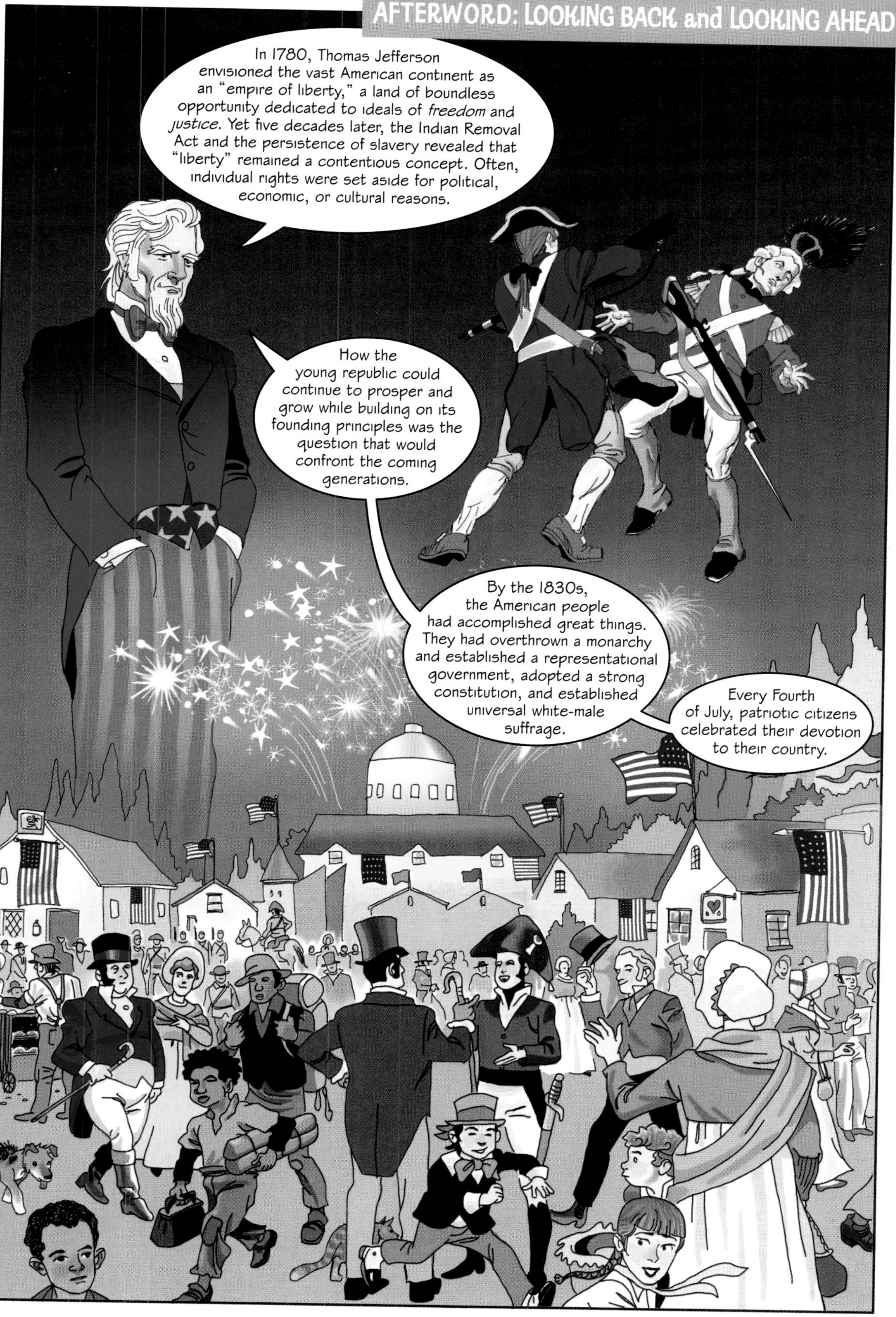
In 1780, Thomas Jefferson envisioned the vast American continent as an "empire of liberty," a land of boundless opportunity dedicated to ideals of *freedom* and *justice*. Yet five decades later, the Indian Removal Act and the persistence of slavery revealed that "liberty" remained a contentious concept. Often, individual rights were set aside for political, economic, or cultural reasons.
How the young republic could continue to prosper and grow while building on its founding principles was the question that would confront the coming generations.
By the 1830s, the American people had accomplished great things. They had overthrown a monarchy and established a representational government, adopted a strong constitution, and established universal white-male suffrage.
Every Fourth of July, patriotic citizens celebrated their devotion to their country.

Already, the United States had doubled in size. Powered by the Industrial Revolution, it began to build huge new transportation and communications systems to link the ever-expanding nation. Throughout the 19th century, Americans would embrace what they thought was their "manifest destiny" to dominate the continent and spread their influence throughout the world.

Yet economic and territorial expansion raised anew questions of justice and equality. National debates raged about abolition, women's rights, and the fate of Native Americans that would determine the identity and future of the Republic.

Elizabeth Cady Stanton

Frederick Douglass

Chief Joseph

The issue of slavery, especially, threatened to tear the Union apart.

Eventually, it would take a savage civil war to resolve the question of whether a "government of the people, by the people, for the people" could endure.

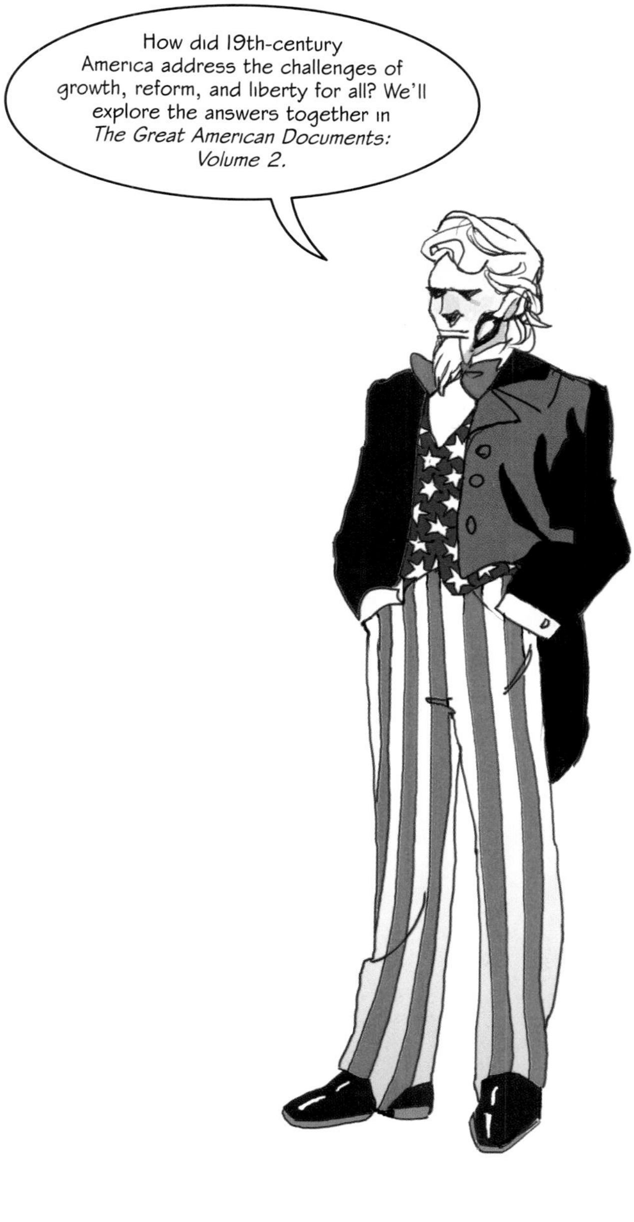
How did 19th-century America address the challenges of growth, reform, and liberty for all? We'll explore the answers together in *The Great American Documents: Volume 2.*

Aaronson, Marc. *The Real Revolution: The Global Story of American Independence.* New York: Clarion, 2005.

Alderman, Ellen, and Caroline Kennedy. *In Our Defense: The Bill of Rights in Action.* New York: Harper, 1992.

Ambrose, Stephen J. *Undaunted Courage: Meriwether Lewis, Thomas Jefferson, and the Opening of the American West.* New York: Simon & Schuster, 1996.

Beeman, Richard. *The Penguin Guide to the United States Constitution.* New York: Penguin, 2010.

Blumberg, Rhoda. *What's the Deal? Jefferson, Napoleon, and the Louisiana Purchase.* Washington, D.C.: National Geographic Society, 1998.

————. *The Incredible Journey of Lewis and Clark.* New York: HarperCollins, 1987.

Doherty, Kiernan. *Puritans, Pilgrims, and Merchants: Founders of the Northeastern Colonies.* Minneapolis, MN: The Oliver Press, 2000.

Ehle, John. *The Trail of Tears: The Rise and Fall of the Cherokee Nation.* New York: Anchor, 1988.

Ellis, Joseph. *Founding Brothers: The Revolutionary Generation.* New York: Knopf, 2001.

Faber, Doris and Harold Faber. *The Birth of a Nation.* New York: Scribner's, 1989.

Feelings, Tom. *The Middle Passage.* New York: Dial, 1996.

Fleming, Thomas J. *Liberty!: The American Revolution.* New York: Viking, 1997.

————. *The Louisiana Purchase.* Hoboken, New York: J. Wiley, 2003.

Greenblatt, Miriam. *War of 1812.* New York: Facts on File, 2003.

Hakim, Joy. *A History of Us.* Oxford University Press, Vols I-11. New York: Oxford University Press, 1993–2003.

Hartman, Gary R. *Landmark Supreme Court Cases.* New York: Checkmark Books, 2006.

Haynes, Charles C., Sam Chaltain and Susan M. Glisson. *First Freedoms: A Documentary History of First Amendment Rights in America.* Oxford, UK: Oxford University Press, 2006.

Heidler, David S. and Jeanne T. Heidler. *The War of 1812.* Westport, CT: The Greenwood Press, 2002.

Hennessey, Jonathan and Aaron McConnell. *The United States Constitution: A Graphic Adaptation.* New York: Hill and Wang, 2008.

Horton, James Oliver and Lois E. Horton. *Slavery and the Making of America.* Oxford, UK: Oxford University Press, 2005.

Kiernan, Denise and Joseph D'Agnese. *Signing Our Rights Away: The Fame and Misfortune of the Men Who Signed the Constitution.* Philadelphia: Quick Books, 2011.

————. *Signing Our Lives Away: The Fame and Misfortune of the Men Who Signed the Declaration of Independence.* Philadelphia: Quick Books, 2009.

King, Jonathan. *The Mayflower Miracle: The Pilgrim's Own Story of the Founding of America.* London: David & Charles, 1987.

Lewis, Anthony. *Freedom for the Thought that We Hate: A Biography of the First Amendment.* New York: Basic Books, 2007.

Lough, Loree. *Lord Baltimore: English Politician and Colonist.* New York: Chelsea House, 2000.

Mack, Stan. *Taxes, the Tea Party, and Those Revolting Rebels: A History in Comics of the American Revolution.* New York: NMB, 2012.

Marrin, Albert. *George Washington and the Founding of a Nation.* New York: Dutton, 2001.

————. *The War for American Independence: The Story of the American Revolution.* New York: Atheneum, 1988.

————. *The Struggle for a Continent: The French and Indian Wars, 1690–1760.* New York: Atheneum, 1987.

————. *1812: The War Nobody Won.* New York: Atheneum, 1985.

McCullough, David. *1776.* New York: Simon & Schuster, 2005.

Miller, John, ed. *The Complete History of American Slavery.* San Diego, CA: Greenhaven Press, 2001.

Molotsky, Irvin. *The Flag, the Poet and the Song: The Story of the Star-Spangled Banner.* New York: Dutton, 2001.

Monk, Linda R. *The Constitution: The Words We Live By: Your Annotated Guide to the Constitution.* New York: Hyperion, 2004.

Our Documents: 100 Milestone Documents from the National Archives. New York: Oxford University Press, 2003.

Philbrick, Nathaniel. *Mayflower.* New York: Penguin, 2006.

Rakove, Jack N. *The Annotated U.S. Constitution and Declaration of Independence.* Cambridge, MA: Harvard University Press, 2009.

Rediker, Marcus. *The Slave Ship.* New York: Viking, 2007.

Sgroi, Peter. *The Living Constitution: Landmark Supreme Court Decisions.* New York: Julian Messner, 1987.

Stewart, Mark. *The Indian Removal Act.* Minneapolis, MN: Compass Point Books, 2007.

Werner, Kirk D., ed. *The American Revolution.* San Diego, CA: Greenhaven Press, 2000.

Zinn, Howard. *A People's History of the United States: 1492–Present.* New York: HarperCollins, 2003.

SUGGESTED WEBSITES AND MULTIMEDIA

Slavery and the Making of America. WNET, 2005. DVD.

National Constitution Center: www.constitutioncenter.org

www.ushistory.org, 1995–2013.

American Masters: www.pbs.org

American Experience: www.pbs.org

Architect of the Capitol: www.aoc.gov

The Library of Congress: www.loc.gov

National Archives: www.archives.gov

The History Channel: www.history.com

The Gilder Lehrman Institute for American History: www.gilderlehrman.org

UNCLE SAM is the most famous personification of the United States of America. Although Sam is rumored to have made his debut appearance in the song "Yankee Doodle Dandy" during the Revolutionary War, he most probably stepped onto the American stage during the War of 1812.

Legend has it that his name derives from one Samuel Wilson, a meat-packer from Troy, New York, who was known locally as Uncle Sam. When Wilson supplied meat to American troops during the War of 1812, he stamped the initials *U.S.* on every package--and soldiers began to associate the term "Uncle Sam" with the United States.

But the Uncle Sam who serves as the symbolic representation of the nation owes his celebrity to two artists. In the middle of the nineteenth century, the editorial cartoonist Thomas Nast popularized what came to be the most familiar image of Uncle Sam, with his goatee, striped pants, and top hat. In the twentieth century, the illustrator James Montgomery Flagg borrowed that image for a World War I and World War II army recruiting poster and created the most famous image of Uncle Sam ever.

So who is Uncle Sam? He is a protective uncle of the people. Over the years he has been portrayed as just, fair, firm, enterprising, and wise. On Uncle Sam Day, designated by Congress in 1989 as September 13, President George H. W. Bush declared that "Uncle Sam recalls the pride and strength of the American people, as well as the freedom we enjoy . . . Today, the figure of Uncle Sam continues to remind us of the great risks and personal sacrifices endured by generations of Americans in the quest for liberty." As a universally recognized spokesman for the United States, Uncle Sam is a natural as the narrator of the country's history.

ACKNOWLEDGMENTS

To Howard Zimmerman, who first imagined that a graphic history of the most important documents of American history could be both fun and educational. His leadership and editorial expertise have been invaluable, and we are most grateful for his friendship and advice.

To Russell Motter, whose encyclopedic knowledge of American history has informed this project from start to finish. Thank you, Russell, for your careful, detailed notes on each chapter and for your suggestions on revision.

To Richard Amari, book designer par excellence, who has proved patient, dedicated, and creative in his interpretation of picture and words.

To Thomas LeBien, who first saw the potential in the idea that Uncle Sam could be the supreme narrator of important American moments in history, and to Amanda Moon and Daniel Gerstle, who have brought this manuscript to fruition at Hill and Wang.

And of course to Jeff Seroy, the best publicist ever.

To our daughter, Becky Ashby-Colón, for her support of our joint effort and for her help with coloring the manuscript.

We would also like to acknowledge Dorothea Ashby, Judith Ashby, Stephen Gutz, Sarah Gutz, Bradley Shotola, Amanda Colón, Luisa Colón, Suzan Colón, and Phil Falino, for their love and encouragement.

A NOTE ABOUT THE AUTHOR AND ILLUSTRATOR

RUTH ASHBY is the author of more than thirty books for children and young adults. A former book editor, she teaches English at Portledge School in Locust Valley, New York. She earned her undergraduate degree in English at Yale University and a master's degree in English literature at the University of Michigan.

ERNIE COLÓN is the illustrator of the *New York Times* bestseller *The 9/11 Report: A Graphic Adaptation*, *After 9/11*, *Che*, and *Anne Frank* (all published by Hill and Wang). He has worked at Marvel and at DC Comics, where he oversaw the production for *Green Lantern*, *Wonder Woman*, *Blackhawk*, and *The Flash*.

Ashby and Colón are happily married and live in Huntington, New York.

A NOTE ABOUT THE EDITORIAL CONSULTANT

RUSSELL MOTTER teaches U.S. history and African American studies at 'Iolani School in Honolulu, Hawaii. He holds a master's degree in history from the University of Hawaii and has done graduate work at Rice University and Columbia University.

COMING SOON

The Great American Documents

VOLUME II: 1831–1900